'Livi's History

"PUBLIC PARKS TO PREMIER LEAGUE"

JOHN AND CAROL BAIN

First published in Great Britain in 2004 by
Carol Bain, West Lothian
ISBN: 0-9547545-0-6

Front cover image and design by the author Carol Bain

Printed in Great Britain by
Hugh K. Clarkson & Sons Limited
- *Commercial & Colour Printers* -
Young Street, West Calder, West Lothian, EH55 8EQ
Tel: 01506 872241 • Fax: 01506 872710 • ISDN: 01506 870236
E-mail: hughclarkson@btconnect.com

ACKNOWLEDGEMENTS

I WOULD ESPECIALLY LIKE TO THANK Amanda Draper of the Museum of Science & Industry in Manchester for her invaluable help researching and collating the old files on Ferranti Limited, the company.

Tony Kinder whose knowledge and help has been second to none. Dominic Keane who has had endless patience and one hundred percent encouragement for me.

Club secretary Jim Renton for his unfailing patience.

Local library assistant and 'Football Mentor' Jackie Stark for her invaluable knowledge, support, and generous help, along with the archetypal club fan Lorraine Kelly for her knowledge and help.

I would also like to express my gratitude to Brian Meek and Jim Pollock of the old Livingston Development Corporation, Bill Robertson, Robin Melrose, Lawrie Glasson in giving access to the scrapbook of his later father Peter Glasson, Alistair Hood, (still with LFC) Tom McLaren, fans liaison officer Kay Robertson, Lorraine and Bobby Wilson and sons, Danny Cunning, Arthur Duncan, Angus Paton, Arthur MacDonald, John Greenhorn, secretary East of Scotland League.

Tom Muir for supplying photographs of Livingston FC, Meadowbank kit man Peter Reynolds, and Hugh Cowan, ex Ferranti player.

Dave Wilkinson from Manchester, and to all those many others who have helped in the making of this book.

This book could not have written however, without the help of my editor, Michael Streeter, formally The Daily Mirror, Daily Mail, The Independent, The Independent on Sunday, and former Editor of the Daily Express in Glasgow.

Last but not least, I would like to thank my family, husband Ian, daughter Samantha, and son Christopher for all their support, and encouragement. My father-in-law John Bain, (the real storyteller) one of the men who helped to make the Ferranti dream come true, and who has been patient, dignified and helpful in equal measure.

To some who are no longer with us but gave unfailing support while they were.

Carol Bain, *Author.*

Contents

FOREWORD

I ALWAYS FEEL THAT HISTORY is a compelling magnet particularly football as it draws on your emotions and nostalgia. Whoever you supported as a boy never leave you as your life is usually woven into the fabric of the Club through all your family links from Grandfather, Father, Uncles and cousins. It is also romantic when we can trace the beginnings of the smaller clubs through to its present day station, as is the case in Livingston Football club and people like John Bain.

There are John Bains everywhere, solid honest hardworking trustworthy servants whose pride in their football club over-rides all other aspects of their life. I first met John when he was chairman of Meadowbank Thistle formerly Ferranti Thistle and could not have been more impressed by his demeanour. I was also aware of his service to the Club for many years through from Ferranti to Livingston F.C. and it is the John Bains of this world who we all can admire. What Livingston have achieved under the present structure with Dominic Keane, Willie Haughey, Jim Leishman and Davie Hay is truly amazing. They have brought a real ambition and drive to the Club, Premier League and UEFA Cup football. Goodness, this is the stuff that dreams are made of and I don't think the dream is over.

I am confident that Livingston will go on from here and establish themselves as a modern and thriving club, which has given its community hope and inspiration. I am sure this read will evoke many happy memories for all those who have traces of the Club in their hearts whether in its early days on now and yes maybe even a few tears.

Enjoy it!

Alex. Ferguson

Sir Alex Ferguson C.B.E.

Introduction

ITTLE DID ANYONE REALISE WHEN the first building blocks were laid on the site at Crewe Toll, Edinburgh, in the spring of 1943 the significance the name Ferranti would play in the Scottish community. All effort was concentrated on the vital task of producing the thousands of gyro gunsights needed for our aircraft for the D-Day invasion, but when this had been successfully achieved, thoughts turned to making Crewe Toll into a centre of advanced technology. What an impact our small works team has made on the history of Scottish football.

Over the years the name Ferranti has been replaced by, first, GEC Marconi and then BAe SYSTEMS. This is a feature of the world we live in, where takeovers and mergers drive and shape our business identity. What we haven't lost in this process are the original values that created and drove us to be a respected innovator in various technologies and a market leader in radar.

In this sense our 'works team' has progressed in a similar vein. Started by individuals whose goals were visionary, albeit within the context of the local leagues they played in, they, in progressing, recognised the need for change and have transformed themselves from the team that played 'across the road from the factory' as Ferranti Thistle to Livingston Football club with the very modern stadium at Almondvale. It is very heartening that solid, well thought out plans are in place to take the team further.

In the world of technology, innovation and change are not the only ever present ingredients; they are in fact mandatory requirements. Likewise, Livingston football club is showing the way to other football clubs in their innovative approach, particularly in their off field and community activities.

Ferranti as a business developed many international markets, and it's Edinburgh factories developed products that are in worldwide use today and will be well into the future. It was with great pride that we followed our team in their first international adventure, however short, and I hope that this adventure will soon be resumed.

This book traces the history and the contributions made by those visionaries many years ago. It also documents the hard work it took to get Livingston Football Club to where it is today. It is with great pride that we can say, we in Ferranti contributed to the making of history in a field that none of us ever imagined.

Graham Russell, *Operations and Site Director, BAe SYSTEMS*
Sir Donald McCallum, *former General Manager, Ferranti, Edinburgh*

PREFACE

THE STORY OF LIVINGSTON FC is no 'Roy of the Rovers' schoolboy tale; this is fact. What team could compare? It should never be forgotten that without a successful 'Ferranti Thistle' there would never have been a 'Meadowbank Thistle' and therefore no 'Livingston' and the fairytale would never have been realised.

My involvement with Livingston FC goes back to 1952 when I joined Ferranti Limited and played with their team in the welfare League. The war years had seen me stationed in Portsmouth with the Royal Navy, but this did not stop my football career. I continued playing for clubs such as Portsmouth and Reading, and it therefore seemed to be a natural progression to continue this on leaving the Navy.

On returning after the end of the war, Ferranti Limited was considered the dynamic aeronautics company and I joined them as a planning engineer/production foreman in one of the machine shops. At the same time, I became involved with the works football team. There appeared to be a lot of potential in developing this small band of men, many of whom were also just back from the war. The next 23 years saw me going from player to manager and board member.

At the start of the 1970s, we applied to become members of the Scottish Football Association (SFA) our membership was delayed due to SFA requirements about our ground at City Park and the support we received at that time from men like Bill Lindsay, the then Chairman of Heart of Midlothian; Tom Hart and Tommy Younger of Hibernian; and Tom Devlin, Director of Celtic, legends in their own right, was unfaltering and unquestionable. These people were all administrators of the SFA and SFL, as well as their respective clubs. I don't think the same help and assistance we received then would be given to a minor club today.

After a successful season in 1973-74, when we won the qualifying Cup (South), we applied along with several other clubs to join the Scottish football league. We eventually won the ballot and joined the second division of the SFL, in 38th place. Caley Thistle was one of the teams we defeated in the ballot, hence the rivalry between the teams going right back to that time.

Our jubilation was short lived, though, as we were then given just six weeks in which to change our name and ground. The SFA could not allow us to join the League while using the name of a commercial company in our title. Of course, 'Sponsorship' was a dirty word in those days – how times have changed!

We had an up and down time both on and off the park while at our new home. Meadowbank Stadium, which was the ground offered to us by the City council if we agreed to include the name 'Meadowbank' in our name? Among the highlights were winning the Second division Championship in 1986-87 and coming second in the First Division the next year. Quite an achievement for a part time team with no real fan base and which was run on a 'shoestring'.

The turning point for the club (Meadowbank Thistle) in the early 1990s was the intervention of Bill Hunter and his board at the time, of which I was a member, who had the foresight to move the club Livingston, West Lothian. Without this move we would never have achieved the heights of the Premier League or European football, and credit must be given to Dominic Keane, who took over in 1995 and transformed this club into a force to be reckoned with.

Many other clubs have reached this status, although probably not many have had such a turbulent history as Ferranti Thistle/Meadowbank Thistle FC and that's what makes this rise so unique.

What also makes this club stand out is the close, almost family like, relationship with their fans. This type of following and commitment is still a major part of Livingston FC today. Many famous names are associated with the club, including DJ John Peel, and one of our most ardent supporters is a friend of long standing, Sir Alex Ferguson,. An inspiration not only to thousands, possibly millions, around the world but also to myself, he is considered by many people to be one of the most successful football club managers of all time. Winning European trophies with both Scottish and English clubs, his achievements have given other smaller clubs the motivation to follow his management approach.

Other fans, not so well known but equally important, included the couple who, although registered blind, regularly made the 800 mile round trip from their home in Surrey to support the team.

For myself, I have my own personal scrapbook to look back on over all these years, from player, to manager and director, and now honorary vice president. It is still a thrill for me to stand in the crowd time after time and feel the excitement, to feel the adrenalin surge and the pride of being part of this wonderful club and the people that are taking the game to it's peak.

John Bain, BEM, *honorary Vice president of Livingston Football Club.*

I

FERRAПTI THISTLE – THE EARLY YEARS

◆

IT WAS A LOW-KEY AND unusual announcement for the start of a footballing dream. 'New factory' proclaimed *The Evening Dispatch* on 17 June 1943, adding that its construction on a Scottish site had been completed in 111 days. The accompanying article, its author doubtless mindful of wartime restrictions on giving valuable information to the enemy, was hardly more illuminating. True, it revealed that this factory had cost more than £100,000, and would bring employment for 1,250 Scots. But other than providing some facts about how it was built, and the number of bricks used (1.25 million apparently), the newspaper gave few details about the factory. This reticence also extended to what the new plant was planning to manufacture. Even the identity of the person who opened the plant was kept secret. The newspaper delicately reported: ' "This is a very important civic occasion," declared the personage who performed the ceremony.'

The secrecy was understandable, given the true nature of the factory. It had been sited in Scotland, as part of the Government's policy of ensuring military-related industry was widely dispersed – and thus less vulnerable to enemy attack. The new plant, located at Crewe Toll on Ferry Road in northwest Edinburgh, was in fact to develop and build a new type of gun sight – called the gyro gun sight – for Allied aircraft.

Though the Government had helped sponsor the building of the factory, the new owners and the makers of this crucial piece of aircraft gunnery were a private company from England, a firm who were new to the area. The Ferranti name had arrived in Scotland.

The arrival may have been anonymous, but Ferranti was soon a major player in Edinburgh life; it marked the start of a fifty-year presence by the firm, during which the company blazed a trail in defence and avionic production in the country and started a boom in defence and aeronautic engineering. That was not all. The new Ferranti factory was also to prove the catalyst for a Scottish footballing fairy tale. Sixty years and two name changes later, the heirs to the company's recreational football team Ferranti Thistle are still playing as a team. Only now, this team has swapped the comfortable obscurity of the welfare leagues for Scotland's Premier League and are rubbing shoulders with some of Europe's finest players in the UEFA Cup. They are the Lions of Livingston, the heirs of the Ferranti dream.

The Ferranti Company was established by the precocious British-born inventor and industrialist Dr Sebastian Ziani de Ferranti in 1882 when he was barely eighteen. Within five years, Sebastian's vision was behind the development of the world's first high-voltage power station at Deptford in south-east London. From its early days Ferranti Limited was based in Hollinwood, Oldham and Manchester though later had outlets in Canada and elsewhere in the world as well as a small workforce in London. After Sebastian's death in 1930, his son Vincent – later Sir Vincent – took over the running of the family firm. Its business was diverse. The company's plants produced a range of domestic electrical appliances, including cookers and irons, and electric meters as well as making munitions during World War One and again for the British Admiralty in the 1930's. Ferranti also had an Instrument Division that made instruments for aircraft. It was this last speciality that led the British Government to ask Ferranti to help in developing the new Gyro Gun Sight (GGS).

Edinburgh was chosen for the location of the new factory not just because of the Government's desire to spread industry around the United Kingdom during war time, but also because it possessed a sizable and skilled workforce. Work began on the undeveloped site in February 1943, and was swiftly completed by June –by December the first gun sights had been delivered.

The factory's ability to manufacture the gun sights so quickly is said to have had a significant effect on the outcome of the war. The sights made it easier for fighter pilots to shoot to shoot-down German aircraft – the 'kill rate' was increased by up to 50 per cent. Indeed, one expert claimed at the time it was probably the single most important piece of equipment the RAF had introduced during the war.

The new general manager of the plant was John (later Sir John) Toothill who had thrown himself into designing and overseeing the factory with enthusiasm. The same was not true of the other nineteen staff who were moved up from Manchester to help with the start of this new project. The company had to come up with some financial inducements to persuade them to go, and had to promise that all the Manchester staff could return home after the wartime emergency was over. Interestingly, none of them would later choose to do so.

Despite the wartime success of the Crewe Toll plant, the Ferranti link with Scotland could have ended as abruptly as it had started. After the war ended in 1945, and the highly motivated staff had produced some 9,594-gun sights, the immediate future for the Crewe Toll factory looked bleak. Who needed a wartime factory making gun sights now there was peace?

Fortunately, for the staff, as well as Scottish football, the head of the company Vincent Ferranti took an enlightened view of the situation. The Crew Toll site could stay open, he declared – as long as it could find a way to make a profit in the post-war environment. John Toothill, already fond of his new Scottish home, was determined to ensure it did just that. In the coming years the Edinburgh site turned its collective hand to a number of products, including cooker switches, transformers for deaf aids and even – with the apparent involvement of the author Enid Blyton – what were called 'Mini Cine' slide projectors for children. The future lay, however, in the aeronautics and defence industries and the production of specialist aircraft instruments and radar. (By a delicious quirk of fate the old Ferranti site off Ferry Road is now occupied by BAe Systems, who are sponsors of Livingston FC, and thus involved with the heirs of the Ferranti Thistle mantle.) Soon the workforce at Ferranti's Scottish plant were making a name for themselves as technically accomplished and productive staff. And it was not long before the workforce began to get noticed in the sporting arena as well.

The term 'Ferranti spirit' had come to be used to describe the firm's innovative approach to industry and its 'can do' attitude. It also summed up the community ethos of the workforce. Sport and recreation – as well as education – were already hallmarks of Ferranti's two major plants at Moston and Hollinwood in the north-west of England and this approach to communal life was soon developed in the Crewe Toll site as well. Even before the Second World War the company had held the Ferranti Transatlantic Cup (later Trophy), a golfing contest between the rival Manchester sites and one at Toronto, Canada, too. These matches were played simultaneously (or as near as possible allowing for the time difference) and the players' net scores were then compared to determine the trophy winner. The event was restored after the war, and in 1946, the Edinburgh staff entered the contest for the first time. They met with little success at the first attempt, but just a year later the trophy was won by one Alistair Waddell, a Scot who worked in the planning department at Crewe Toll. Waddell, who played off a handicap of three, shot a net 69 at the Number 2 course at Gullane Golf Club near Edinburgh. The Ferranti staff in Scotland were already on the sporting map. Yet though staff at Ferranti were to continue to excel at golf and also chess in future years, it was in another activity that the firm was really to make its mark on the Edinburgh social landscape – football.

Just exactly when and where a team called Ferranti Thistle played a competitive fixture for the first time is unclear. Documentation during that period was rare – in part due to paper rationing at the end of the war – and personal recollections of that time are now fading.

The team may have had its first informal kick around as early as 1943 when the workforce first started at the site. Certainly interest in sport seems to have increased soon after the end of the war, as Ferranti switched to peacetime work and as young men returned to the area from active service and found apprenticeships and employment at the firm. The Crewe Toll site had its own recreation area, and across the Ferry Road there stood a makeshift sports ground with two old army huts used as changing rooms. The location was far from ideal – it also had to be used for cricket, rugby union and bowls as well as football – but it was a start for the keen young staff at Ferranti. The side and its organisation grew out of the Recreation Club, which from the earliest days at Crewe Toll was the hub of social and sporting activity at Ferranti, and was to remain closely associated with the footballing success for many years. The Recreation clubhouse was called the Bon Ami, and was not just the central point of decision making about the football side – but also the scene of many lively social gatherings.

So it was that at some point in the mid-1940's a team from the quickly-flourishing Ferranti site joined one of the local Welfare Leagues that were popular at the time and made their way into Scottish football legend as Ferranti Thistle. The names of the teams who Ferranti played against in the Lothian Welfare League make fascinating reading – Leith Dockers, Arnot Mcleod Builders and Nelson Printers to name just a few. All the teams and their players were competitive in the welfare league, though few would have the determination and organisation to carry on to greater heights as a club. Ferranti Thistle did develop that drive – and that was largely due to some key characters who joined the team in its early days.

Derek Read had worked at the Ferranti plant at Hollinwood, Oldham, and had done his national service while apprenticed there. A keen footballer, Derek's life changed forever soon after the end of the war when he met his wife-to-be Betty, and decided to move to Scotland to be with her. He moved to the plant at Crewe Toll as a fitter and was soon heavily involved in the emerging Ferranti Thistle works team.

Derek typified the early spirit of the club, a spirit that drove Ferranti on from its modest beginnings to what it would ultimately achieve as a fully professional team. He was passionate about football, and a decent player on the left wing, but he also displayed the hard-work and organisation skills to make sure the team developed. When the works side set up an organising committee to put the team on a serious footing, Derek was one of the key members of that body. It admittedly helped Derek and the rest of the committee that the Ferranti board – in keeping with their desire to encourage an *esprit de corps* among the workforce – gave their full backing to the team's efforts to improve themselves.

Another key member of the playing and organising team in these pioneering times was Tommy Learmouth, who had also joined Ferranti as an employee in the early 1940's. Like Derek, Tommy was a good organisational man and someone dedicated enough to devote much of his spare time to the game and the team he loved. Later, Tommy was to become a representative on the board of the East of Scotland Football Association, a tribute to his administrative skills.

It was through the hard work of such men as Derek Read, Tommy Learmouth and others, combined with the natural footballing talent of the Ferranti workforce that Ferranti Thistle started to earn good reviews as a decent football outfit. Hard work, team spirit, and determination on the pitch were the key qualities of Thistle in those early days. They had to be. They may have been backed by one of Scotland's more dynamic companies but there was nothing inevitable about their rise to top flight football.

There are, frustratingly, no reports of Ferranti's matches in those Welfare League days, and we can only guess at their style of play, their formation, or even who rattled in the goals up front.

There is, however, one tantalising glimpse of an early Ferranti game in 1949, when the Edinburgh works team took on not one of their Welfare League rivals but their English colleagues from down in Manchester and Oldham. The friendly rivalry between the two main plants at Hollinwood and Moston and the one at Crewe Toll had already been kindled by the Ferranti Transatlantic Trophy in golf – a tournament in which the Scots had had more than their fair share of success. The English employees, however, were determined not to be outdone by their Scottish colleagues when it came to other sports.

So it was on Saturday 14 May 1949, that 42 members of the Hollinwood and Moston sports team made the long trek up by train to Edinburgh to take part in a sports event with their friends in the north. Still bleary-eyed from their early train, the English contingent received a warm welcome from greeters from the Scottish plant. They were soon whisked off in buses to the Crewe Toll canteen for breakfast, before a sightseeing tour of the city – including the obligatory visit to the Castle and Hollyrood – followed by lunch at a city centre restaurant.

The real business began at 2pm with the sports meeting held at Ferranti's own playing grounds at Crewe Toll.

The event started with a netball match between the women from Hollinwood and Moston against the female staff from Crewe Toll. The result was never in doubt, with the English side winning comfortably 14 goals to 4.

The football match which followed between the men from the rival plants was a different matter however. The players from Moston and Hollinwood took their football seriously and had every reason to be confident of beating their Scottish rivals. The northwest was then, as it remains today, one of the strongholds of English football. Indeed, eleven years later a Ferranti engineering side from Manchester entered the Chorlton League and won it at the first attempt; meanwhile a direct descendant of that team – East Manchester FC – plays in the very competitive Manchester league today. However, the Edinburgh Ferranti team had no intention of simply making up the numbers against the English team. By half time, the score was 2-0 to the home side, and though the English outfit pulled one goal back in the second half, Ferranti Thistle ran out 2-1 winners. The victory must have been a huge morale booster for the Scottish team and a blow for the Manchester staff who took such pride in their sport. None of this emotion, however, was conveyed in the brief match report that ran in the in-house Ferranti Journal, which was edited, from the Hollinwood site by RGB Gwyer. It simply noted: 'The Scottish side led by 2-0 at half-time, but a goal scored by R. Howarth in the second half gave the final result – Edinburgh 2 Manchester 1'. The report added: 'Mr A. Watt, Scottish Referee Supervisor and an international referee, controlled the game.'

The journal made no mention of the Scottish players who scored, though they were Derek Read and Ted Lowry. Nevertheless the Oldham-based Journal was gracious enough to commend the Edinburgh staff for 'some real Scottish hospitality' which later included a Recreation Club Dance at Masonic Hall in Forth Street, followed by a late train home at 11pm. Clearly the rail service was rather better in those days than it is now.

If the Manchester side was looking for revenge when 32 men and women from Crewe Toll travelled down to Oldham in September later that same year 1949, they were to be bitterly disappointed. The Edinburgh staff made a weekend of the break, travelling down on Friday 23 September and not returning until Sunday. In between the Scottish netball term were soundly beaten 24-6, but once more Thistle – the name emphasised the Scottishness of the side – ran out 2-1 winners over their English rivals in the football match. Yet again, the Ferranti Journal gives us no clue as to who were the stars of the Thistle side or who scored the winning goals.

These contests between the men and women of Edinburgh and Oldham and Manchester became regular twice-yearly events. Not only were they fun sporting occasions, but they also fostered lasting friendships and even love affairs and marriage between staff from the two Ferranti sites.

It is hard to escape the conclusion, however, that the editor of the Ferranti Journal was a little embarrassed at the superiority of the Scottish football team. The Journal records another of the meeting between the sides on 13 May 1950, but it curiously neglects to mention what the outcome of this game was. And after that the Journal remains quiet on further meetings between the two rival camps.

If Thistle were having success against their friendly rivals and colleagues down south, then this was mirrored in the welfare league. During their few years in the Lothian Welfare League, Ferranti picked up no fewer than six trophies – no small achievement and a sign that they were beginning to outgrow their time in junior football. By 1952 the company was beginning to flex its commercial muscles and had already become the second largest industrial employer in Scotland and the largest in the electronics sector. The works football team was also, it seems, ready to move on to bigger and better achievements. This move was helped at the time by the arrival of a new face at Ferranti, John Bain. John had been in the Royal Navy during the Second World War and had been stationed at Portsmouth on the south coast of England. A keen and talented footballer, he played both for Portsmouth and Reading as both outside left and left back. As a lad he could have signed professionally for Hearts, but his mother insisted he got a 'proper job' instead. Hearts' loss was to be Ferranti's gain. When John returned to Edinburgh in 1952, he came to work for the company as a planning engineer and production foreman in one of the machine shops. Naturally he quickly gravitated towards the football team. The Thistles already had the commitment of stalwarts such as Derek Read and Tommy Learmouth to encourage them to raise their standards. Now the arrival of such a quality player as John Bain and his sharp football brain was yet another step forward in the fledgling club's progress. He quickly established himself as a star player and soon afterwards as manager of the team.

However men such as Derek Read and John Bain were not always able to plan events as well as they might have liked.

An example was the occasion in the early 1950's when Derek and his committee decided it was time for Ferranti to have their own dedicated kit. After all, if they were going to try to make it big as a team, they might as well try and look the part. As usual, Derek organised a collection before dispatching two members of the team to Thornton's sports shop in Princes Street to buy a kit for the team to wear. It was one of the very few outlets at the time where sports kit could be found. Unfortunately, by the time the pair arrived at the shop there was only one strip still available. This had been ordered by another team but which had not been collected. The snag was, it was a rugby team who had made the order – and so this was a rugby strip. Undeterred, the two Thistle men paid for the shirts, shorts and socks, and hurried back off to where the committee was waiting to review the purchase. The colour of the strip, of course, was gold and black – team colours that have endured down the intervening decades despite being chosen completely by accident was back in the 1950's. . But then, that is often how traditions start. And at least, as they had bought a rugby team's kit, they had a few spare shirts left over.

Kit issues aside, it was clear that Ferranti were ready for the jump into senior football. They now had a solid team, with John Bain leading the playing side and Derek Read and Tommy Learmouth driving the team's committee forward. It was at this point that Ferranti Thistle took the bold step of applying to join the East of Scotland League.

The East of Scotland League was a formidable league in the early 1950's – as it still is – and made up of strong amateurs sides with a few semi-professional players as well. The list of teams who played in this competitive group at the time included Eyemouth United, Berwick Rangers Reserves, Civil Service Strollers, Chirnside United, Coldstream, Duns, Edinburgh University, Gala Fairydean, Hawick Royal Albert, Murrayfield Amateurs, Peebles Rovers, Selkirk, Spartans and Vale of Leithen. Many of these teams still compete in the League's Premier or First Division to this day.

Membership of this league was a huge step up for Ferranti, who had been used to sweeping most if not all before them in the welfare leagues. Now, not only did they have to face the big boys from the senior league, they also had the prospect one day of entry to the Scottish Football Association and therefore also the Scottish Cup.

On the other hand, the club felt that the step up would allow them to introduce a few semi-professional players into the team, which would allow Ferranti to develop more quickly as a football team. The recreation club, however, still kept a close eye on who did and did not play for the team – the last thing they wanted to do as they entered a bigger league was to lose the sense of camaraderie and team spirit that had brought them this far.

It was thus an exhilarating but nerve-racking moment when Thistle were admitted to the East of Scotland League for the 1953/54 season. Ferranti Thistle had indeed arrived. Players and supporters alike, however, could not help wondering the same thing: could this humble factory works team now make the grade at senior non-league football?

The early signs for Thistle were not good. Their first senior match was against Eyemouth United, a team with whom Ferranti were to have many tussles over the coming years. To make matters harder, the game was away at Eyemouth's forbidding Gunsgreen Park. Their baptism into senior football could hardly have been harder. The game took place on 15 August 1953. In the circumstances, Thistle's 3-1 defeat was perhaps no disgrace. Thistle's scorer was centre forward Ted Lowry. Star performers in the side included John Bain and another man who would become a stalwart of the club Bill Mill – who played on the right wing – plus goalkeeper Frankie Robinson. Others included Bobby Leishman – no relation to his namesake Jim – and Chick Cannon, who still watches Livingston play.

If that poor start was not altogether unexpected, what happened in the following weeks *was* a blow to morale. The big fish of the welfare league had turned into the minnows of the senior league and it was not a pleasant experience to see them being gobbled up by the East of Scotland sharks, either for the players or the band of loyal fans and fellow Ferranti staff. September came and went, and still Ferranti had not recorded their first win at this level. Had this ambitious little works team finally got out of their depth?

However, when management and players alike could have been forgiven for despairing, Ferranti's fortune finally changed in October – and with a vengeance. Not content with grinding out a tedious 1-0 win to gain that first senior win, Thistle turned up and thrashed Chirnside 7-2. The win was a huge morale booster for the team, and showed that their move up to a higher level was certainly justified. The new club could breathe a little more easily now.

The rest of the season was far from easy, but at least Ferranti knew now they could perform at this level. They recorded six wins out of 26 matches, an acceptable return for a first season in senior football. The youthful team, led by John Bain and Bill Mill, had also gained a great deal of experience. Ferranti had proved to themselves and the rest of the world that while they might have been the newest kids on the block, they were here to stay.

It would be fair to say that the rest of the 1950's were, for Ferranti, ones of consolidation, though this was not always a quiet process. Indeed, some of the results were quite spectacular. Thistle were thrashed 9-2 at the start of the 1954/55 season by Coldstream. A few months later, in January 1955, Ferranti beat Chirnside by the incredible scoreline 7-5. Watching Ferranti might be nerve-racking or sometimes downright heart wrenching, but it was rarely boring.

Like most teams at the time Ferranti played with two full-backs, a centre-half, a right half, left half and then five forwards in a fluid style.

The Sixties started off in depressing fashion for Ferranti, with the team losing to their old adversaries Eyemouth by the humiliating scoreline of 11-0. It was a footballing low for Ferranti, and a reminder that despite the progress the club had made, its survival in the more senior flights of football were still not assured.

The biggest threat to Ferranti's senior status, however, came not on the pitch but in the committee room. In the early 1960's Ferranti had set up a youth team to complement the senior side. The idea was that the young Ferranti apprentices, who would wear the badge and blazers of the club (and the company), would become imbued with corporate and club pride and that this would encourage the development of an even greater team spirit around the club – as well as providing a natural feeder team for the senior side.

The new club committee, now headed by John Bain and Bill Mill who had replaced Derek Read and Tommy Learmouth, enthusiastically backed the idea. The youth team was set up with its own committee and Ferranti prided themselves on another step towards the future progress of the club.

Ferranti player Johnny Meikle was one of the members of the new committee handling the youth team, while young Ferranti apprentices who were to play for them included Ian Bain (John's son, who was to play for the senior side in the early 1970's) Norrie Beddingham and Bobby Duncanson. Such of the camaraderie of these players and their workmates that they still, many years later, meet up for regular meetings with other Ferranti apprentices.

However, the under 21 youth team and its committee at that time were to become something of a Trojan horse. There was evidently a feeling among some members of the Ferranti club that they were perhaps over-reaching themselves. The fund-raising needed to keep pace with the demands of senior football – dances, raffles for example – was incessant and demanding. Perhaps, thought the doubters, Ferranti should lower their horizons and end their quest for ever-higher status. The split was between those who came from a strong perhaps semi-professional football background and who were fiercely competitive and ambitious for the team, and those who saw football as more of a social event – a relaxation away from the rigours of daily working life. This latter approach came to be associated with people involved with the youth team and its own organising structure.

So it was not altogether a surprise when the youth team committee put forward the dramatic proposal that the new youth team and the senior team should merge into one – and play in a junior league instead of the senior league where Ferranti now played. The proposal inevitably caused controversy and for a while threatened to split the club into two. If adopted, the proposal meant that the works team would be turning its back on all the progress it had made since its formation after the war. On the other hand, life would be simpler and junior football would place fewer financial and administrative demands on the club.

The proposal was put to a vote of members of the football club at a tense meeting chaired by John Bain, and under the auspices of the Recreation Club, which had maintained its close connection with the football teams. The vote was close, with many voting for the merger option and the effective end of Ferranti's senior football aspirations. However, John Bain ruled that what was termed the 'rebel faction' did not have the necessary two-thirds majority to change the aims of the club, and so the proposal was defeated. Thistle had overcome one of the most serious threats so far to their ambitions as a football club.

The relief provided by this narrow decision made itself felt back on the pitch. The 1962/63 season saw Ferranti claim their first senior trophy when they lifted the East of Scotland Qualifying Cup after beating Gala Fairydean 3-2, with two goals from Colin Brown and the third from Dougie Birrell.

The team who lifted the trophy were managed by John Bain and included Lawrie Glasson (later to be part of the coaching team) John McGonagle, John Craig, Hugh Cowan, Malcolm Angus, Robin Melrose, Jim Lawrence, Dougie Birrell, Colin Brown (Goalie), Brian Teasdale and Hugh McTiernan. This may not have been the most prestigious event in Scottish football but for John Bain, Bill Mill and other senior members of the club this was concrete proof that Ferranti Thistle could not just survive in senior football but flourish as well.

The results of the following seasons largely confirmed this impression. In the 1963/64 season Ferranti beat first Eyemouth (2-0 in a replay) then Gala Fairydean (2-0) in the East of Scotland Qualifying Cup.

One of the biggest games in Ferranti Thistle's history so far took place on 20 April 1964 when they took on Second Division Berwick Rangers in the East of Scotland City Cup Final. This was the first time Ferranti had played League opposition in a competitive match and it was bound to give a good indication of how far this small works team had travelled on the road to football's heights. The game was played on a Thursday evening – kick off was at 7pm – and took place at Powderhall Stadium, the venue for Edinburgh's greyhound racing. To most people's surprise – not least Berwick's – Ferranti held them to a draw. In the replay, Berwick ran out comfortable 4-0 winners but the performance in the two games and even the result were no disgrace for the Edinburgh works team. There was undoubtedly still a gulf between Ferranti and full League opposition, but little by little, that gap was getting smaller. Another highlight of the season was an 11-1 thrashing of Edinburgh University in an East of Scotland league match.

For the remainder of the 1960's trophy success proved elusive for Thistle. They did play in the final of the King Cup in the 1967/68 season, but were soundly beaten 4-1 at Gala by a lively Coldstream side. Otherwise, the results were acceptable, but with little sign that the club was quite ready yet for the final push onwards a higher status.

The decade in fact ended as it had begun with a major question mark hanging over the future of the club. Once again, the problem was off the pitch – or more specifically the problem *was* the pitch. From the 1940's, Ferranti Thistle had played on the same ground off Ferry Road across the road from the Ferranti site and close to the Bruce Peebles factory. Though far from ideal – it could be a desolate spot and the changing rooms were very basic – the Crewe Toll ground was a settled venue and conveniently close to where the team worked.

Now, though, Edinburgh Corporation wanted to buy the land from the

Recreation Club to provide sporting facilities for a new college – the result is the present Telford College.

For the 1969/70 season Ferranti had to quickly find a new location –or face the possibility of losing their senior status and a place in the East of Scotland League.

The solution was a new venue at another Corporation site, City Park, itself barely three-quarters of a mile away from Ferranti. The ground had a rich football tradition and had once been the home of Edinburgh City before that club's demise – City has since reformed and now plays at Meadowbank Stadium, (another ground that would be of importance in the Ferranti story in the future).

For now, though, the 5,000-capacity City Park location seemed like the ideal answer. There was, however, one more problem. The ground had fallen into disrepair and needed a considerable amount of renovation, which in turn would cost a considerable sum of money – money that the Ferranti football team alone could not possibly find.

Fortunately, the company, by now under the general managership Donald (later Sir Donald) McCallum, came to the rescue. It agreed to finance the necessary work on the changing rooms, including a new hot water system, to make the ground fit for senior football. Thistle were to share the ground with Hibs Colts, Hibernian's third team; such ground shares were quite common at the time. All the ground lacked was a secure fence enclosing the pitch; a fault that was to prove a drawback in the years ahead.

The involvement of Ferranti Limited in funding their team's ground renovation would have come as little surprise to those critics at the time who cast envious eyes at the works team and the powerful company behind it. It was assumed by some that the aeronautical giant had always helped to bankroll the team in this way, giving them a head start over its rivals first in the welfare leagues and then in senior football. In reality, while the Ferranti management had always backed the football side – and John Toothill kept his connections with the team club after his retirement from the firm – this had rarely amounted to financial assistance. The club had run dances and other social events to raise money, it is true, employees of the club would donate a small fraction of their wages towards the running of the club, and this did help to keep the playing side of Ferranti solvent. However, this was purely a voluntary payment and the company made no investment itself, other than allowing its wages department to administer the system.

Meanwhile, responsibility for providing clean kit each week lay with John Bain's wife Cathy – a task that could and often did take up the rest of the weekend after a game. This network of connections between players and the company was a real strength. One of the great benefits for Ferranti was that the team and support staff enjoyed a close-knit relationship, providing a determination and willingness to play for each other that kept them going through some of the darker days. In return, the continuing success of the football team was a great morale booster for work colleagues not just in Scotland but at the English sites too.

In the quarter of a century since the club's modest formation as a works team, Ferranti Thistle had continued to grow and to chase a dream. While other works teams fell by the way, or were content to remain in junior leagues, Ferranti and its band of talented and determined staff sensed they could achieve more. The ultimate dream, of course was to do the unthinkable – and take a works football team into the highest ranks of the Scottish Football League. So far, characters such as John Bain and Bill Mill had helped take to their first taste of senior football in the East of Scotland League. Now, as the Sixties drew to a close, and with the club boasting a new ground, these men began to turn their minds to greater goals. First on the agenda was gaining full membership of the Scottish Football Association. The next was the previously unthinkable step of taking this factory works into the ranks of professional football.

After fewer than 30 years as a club, Ferranti was aiming for the big time.

2

Going Up in the World

OR SOME TIME IT HAD irritated officials and players at Ferranti that they were denied one of the greatest prizes in Scottish football, taking part in the Scottish Cup. To enter that competition a club had first to be accepted as a full member of the Scottish Football Association. Unlike many other clubs in the East of Scotland League, Ferranti were still not full SFA members by the start of the 1970's, thus denying them the potential glory – and income – of a cup run against the biggest teams in domestic football.

By 1970 John Bain, Will Mill, and other senior figures in the club were determined to put an end to this anomaly and win their rightful place within the ranks of the SFA.

The club's enforced move to City Park seemed the ideal time for Ferranti to push for this status. The old Edinburgh City ground – a step up from the former Crewe Toll ground – had a history and tradition that was certainly more fitting for big cup ties. There was, however, one major obstacle to the coveted SFA status. Though the Ferranti Company had generously paid for the upgrading of changing rooms and the installation of new showers at City Park, the ground was still not fully enclosed by fencing as demanded by SFA rules. In fact, one end of the ground was completely open. To put this right would cost a considerable sum – an estimated £1,000 – and this was money that the small works team simply did not have. Behind the scenes, nor could the company afford to find even more money for its works team. Though it was still regarded as an industrial giant in Scotland it was – unbeknown to the outside world – already facing severe financial problems.

This lack of an enclosed area was therefore a serious handicap for Ferranti and one with no obvious solution. Frustratingly, it held up Ferranti's application to join the SFA in the 1969/1970 season, their first at the new ground.

Help, though, was close at hand in the form of Tom Hart, the Chairman of Hibs and just as relevantly in this case a successful Edinburgh builder. There was already a connection between the two very differently sized clubs – Hibernian's third team Hibs Colts shared the ground with Ferranti, after all. Even so, Tom Hart's act of generosity in putting the fencing in place at personal cost was as big-hearted as it was welcome. Doubtless, there was an element of calculation about the decision – Hibs probably reckoned that a successful Ferranti could be a more than useful feeder club for supplying home-grown Edinburgh talent to the bigger club – but that alone did not account for the gesture. Certainly, John Bain and others at Ferranti felt then and still feel a debt of gratitude to Hart's generosity.

However, if Ferranti now felt that with an enclosed ground, SFA status was theirs simply for the asking they were to be disappointed. The club was beginning to learn that nothing in Scottish football is ever quite that simple.

The Byzantine deliberations of the SFA had long baffled and bemused outside observers, as well as a number of those who took part in them. So perhaps Ferranti should not have been too surprised when at a gathering in 1972 the Association announced yet another reason to block full membership to the lowly works team and thus entry to the Scottish Cup for these factory part-timers. The executive and the general purposes committee of the SFA claimed that because Ferranti rented City Park from Edinburgh Corporation they did not have a private ground of their own – and were thus ineligible.

It was a puzzling ruling, and for a number of reasons. For one, Edinburgh City, the previous occupants of City Park in past decades, had been eligible to play in the Scottish Cup, and a number of cup-ties *had* been played there. Indeed, City had even played in the Second Division of the Scottish League. This fairly obvious object to the SFA ruling was forced home at the meeting by Tommy Younger from Hibs; the second intervention by that club on behalf of Ferranti. Meanwhile, Tom Devlin from Celtic made another telling point; just the week before his club had played a major European fixture in the Italian city of Milan on a ground that, too, was rented. Were the SFA really going to impose rules more stringent that those applying into the cream of Italian football?

Less exotically, it was also pointed out that Clyde rented their Shawfield ground from the Greyhound Racing Association.

Perhaps unsurprisingly, the vocal support for Ferranti's application from two of Scottish football's big names proved very persuasive and the SFA committee position crumbled. By a substantial majority – thirty-one members voted for the works team – the SFA council voted for the committee to reconsider their rejection of Ferranti. Afterwards, a relieved John Bain, who was chairman as well as manager of Thistle, made clear his pleasure at the council's vote and singled out the support of Hibs. He told journalists: 'We are glad that the committee are to have a rethink on our application and we're indebted to Mr Younger for pressing our case.'

Bain also explained why Ferranti had felt frustrated at the committee's continued rejection of their claim. 'We applied for full membership of the SFA three years ago [in 1969] but were turned down because the ground was not adequately fenced. With the co-operation of Tom Hart of Hibs, we fenced in the pitch. The SFA sent officials through to inspect it and they seemed satisfied.'

The understandable sense of frustration and grievance felt by people at Ferranti was not to last for much longer. Faced with the overwhelming view of the council members of the SFA, the executive committee had little option but to bow to the inevitable. So it was that in 1972, Ferranti Thistle were finally granted full membership of the Scottish Football Association, a fine achievement for a works team that had only existed for three decades. Ferranti officials celebrated the momentous event with a lavish dinner at the well-known Peacock Restaurant in Granton Harbour – a fish restaurant fittingly owned by Tommy Younger, whose club Hibs had done more than most to help Thistle win their coveted SFA status. As the happy evening wore on, even some of the club stalwarts allowed themselves to dream of future glory ahead in the Scottish Cup.

But first they had to get there. Though the big prize of full membership was, of course, the chance to play in the Scottish Cup, SAF status alone did not guarantee it. First they had to overcome the hurdle of the Scottish Qualifying Cup (South), the competition designed to decide which non-league sides would gain the right to enter the draw for the Scottish Cup proper. With so much at stake for all the clubs, this was no easy competition and many good East of Scotland teams could go for years without making it to the Scottish Cup proper. Fortune seemed to smile on Ferranti, however, as a relatively straightforward path through the qualifying cup began to open up for them.

Their first opponents in the Qualifying Cup in September 1972 were the students of Glasgow University, a useful side as the subsequent 2-2 draw suggests. Perhaps a little complacent, Ferranti could have failed at their very first obstacle against the eager and physical student side. The two sets of players were not the only things to clash – their jerseys did too, and Thistle had to borrow a spare kit from Hibs. However, in the replay at City Park Ferranti, restored to their normal gold and black strip, ran out comfortable winners 5-1. The next opponents were Burntisland, who were also dispatched with relative ease – 4-2 – at Ferranti's home ground. In the semi-finals Ferranti received something of a shock when they were on the wrong end of a 5-0 thrashing by Vale of Leithen, a reminder that they were by no means the strongest team in East of Scotland football. Fortunately, while this heavy defeat was a blow to the pride, it did not get in the way of Ferranti's main aim that season – their semi-final berth had already guaranteed them a place in the first round of the Scottish Cup.

Ferranti had achieved yet another milestone in their short existence. Moreover, by reaching the Scottish Cup at their first attempt, they had justified some of the faith that the bigger clubs – Hibs and Celtic in particular – had implied in their championing of Ferranti's SFA status. Manager John Bain, his officials and players had reason to be pleased with themselves, and it was indeed a proud day for the entire Ferranti Company, including staff down in Manchester. If nothing else, entry into the first round of the cup meant that Ferranti Thistle would be granted the ultimate honour of any aspiring football club – to have their name read out in the results section of BBC TV's *Grandstand*.

The works side's first match in the Cup was against the Borders side Duns. Although this was Ferranti's first time in the Cup, they were expected to win this game against fellow non-leaguers, and they did not disappoint, winning 3-1 at home before a decently sized and partisan crowd of 1,000 at City Park. Inside right Henry Mains scored the first, and a brace of goals from right wing Charlie Crawfield sealed the tie before Duns managed a consolation goal two minutes from time. So far the Edinburgh team's progress had attracted little attention bar the brief mention of their result; to be fair, neither they nor Duns were well-known teams outside their area.

However, this began to change when Ferranti shaped up to their opposition in round two of the cup – Elgin City. Though Elgin were also outside the Scottish League, they were a familiar name and a well-respected Highland league with serious aspirations to become a professional side. Suddenly, the media were beginning to take note of Ferranti, and the spotlight focussed on their clash with the Highland side in January 1973. Part of the attraction was the origin of Ferranti team. The club were still very obviously a factory works side and this was a welcome novelty for jaded football correspondents endlessly seeking a new angle for the Cup. Then there was the obscurity – for as one newspaper columnist asked in the run up to the game (and he was probably not alone): 'Who the dickens are Ferranti Thistle?' The team was predictably and easily cast as the 'minnows' of Scottish football, the small fish who were suddenly playing in the big pond with the big boys.

Yet, Ferranti were certainly not overawed by the attention and the coverage on the eve of what was, to be certain, by the far the biggest game in their history. For one thing, the Edinburgh side were at home, and this meant literally that the two teams were not competing on a level playing field. City Park had a distinct slope from one end to the other, the total differential being rather more than the five feet or so that used to exist at Hibs' Easter Road ground (a slope that has since been removed).

Perhaps more importantly, Ferranti did their homework on the Elgin team. No Thistle official had actually travelled up to watch their cup opponents play – it was after all a five hour drive in those days, time was short and expenses had to be rigorously controlled. But club secretary and Ferranti stalwart Bill Mill revealed in interviews that the well-connected works team had used a network of 'spies' up in the north and had therefore managed to prepare a written dossier on each Elgin player. Ferranti, it seems, were leaving nothing to chance in this historic encounter.

Nor, it seems, were Elgin taking any risks with these upstarts from the capital. It was turning into an unusual experience for the Highland team, as the press cast them for once as the relative giants of a second round cup tie against inferior or at least untested opposition. The last thing this ambitious club wanted was any unfortunate and embarrassing slips against a works team from Edinburgh who until recently had enjoyed almost total obscurity. So it was that Elgin went to the lengths of having Ferranti watched by their former goalkeeper Dave Lawtie. Lawtie was still on the books of the club, but had taken time off to concentrate on his studies at Aberdeen University. His footballing brain was still useful to the Elgin cause, however, and the club had dispatched the tall undergraduate to watch Ferranti in their previous cup match against Duns and to glean as much information on them as he could in the time.

It was perhaps a measure of Elgin's confidence that Club secretary Jim Ross felt happy to make public the key conclusions of Lawtie's dossier on the Edinburgh team. Interestingly, Ross's public remarks betrayed none of the overdone praise that teams nowadays routinely heap upon their opposition. Instead, Ross revealed that the goalkeeper considered Ferranti to be 'one-paced'. Ross added: 'He feels we could make fitness the key, and we'll be gearing our tactics accordingly'. Another weakness, according to Lawtie's report, was that the inexperienced works side could be pressured into making mistakes, and Ross conformed that this too would help form Elgin's game plan.

These remarks helped to underline Elgin City's undoubted sense of superiority as the date of the cup-tie approached. However, their tone contrasted sharply with sports reporters who also had been to see Ferranti; this time on the preceding Saturday against Eyemouth United in an East of Scotland League match at City Park. Thistle won 3-1 and impressed a number of those present with their solid 4-3-3 formation and skilful play. The two players picked out as likely threats to Elgin were centre forward Ian Martin – who scored twice against Eyemouth – and right-winger Charlie Crawford, both of them quick, skilful players. Meanwhile, from the touchline, coach Lawrie Glasson – a playing star of an earlier vintage – was urging his team to 'play football, Ferranti'. All in all, the works team made a decent impression.

One writer, Colin Farquharson, was certainly pleasantly surprised by what he had seen, stating that Thistle displayed a 'higher standard of play than I would have expected in the East of Scotland League. Although the slope is tailor-made for "kick and rush tactics" there was very little of the big boot about their play,' he added.

As the day of the cup-tie – 13 January 1973 – approached, so did the excitement surrounding this unpredictable match. The Ferranti 'family' was certainly excited at the presence of one of its teams in the second round of the Scottish Cup, and messages of goodwill and support came in from different parts of the company empire. These included a telex from Sebastian de Ferranti, grandson of the founder of the company and the then chairman. His message to manager John Bain on the eve of the game was: 'THE FERRANTI FAMILY AND ALL OF US HERE AT HOLLINWOOD ARE PROUD OF YOUR ACHIEVEMENTS IN THE SCOTTISH CUP. ALL GOOD WISHES FOR YOUR SUCCESS TOMORROW – AND IN THE NEXT ROUND. S.Z. DE FERRANTI.'

It was a touching reminder of the team's status as a works side and also of the spirit, determination and positive outlook that this fed into the football team.

The excitement notched up another level, too, when the day before the cup tie, Hearts' home League match against Morton was called off because of an outbreak of flu among the Greenock team's players. This late postponement meant that the Ferranti/Elgin clash would be what one newspaper described as the only 'big game' in Edinburgh that afternoon. The scene was set for a thrilling encounter.

In pre-match remarks in Ferranti's modest programme, manager John

Bain set out his team's approach not just to the Elgin game but their philosophy when it came to football. He commented: 'The reputation of Elgin City as a cup team has not gone unnoticed, and we know our task today is no easy one, but our players and committee are not overawed by the importance of the occasion, and I'm sure, if the supporters turn out, our young side will give a good account of themselves. They do not play defensive football, they like to attack, and that is what the game is all about.'

These were positive words, but Bain had every right to feel confident in his side's ability to cope with this step up in standards. . Though it was young, there was still some useful experience in the side; goalkeeper Brian Simpson had played for Dundee, right back Alan McDonald had a spell with Dundee United while Jimmy Thomson had experience with Arbroath. Meanwhile Ferranti's substitute for the day, the 6ft-plus centre-half Allan Robertson had been with both Third Lanark and Hibs.

The full team that day was Simpson, McDonald, Sivewright, Bell, Brock, Nisbet, Crawford, Thomson, Mains, Martin, and Birrell. As this eleven walked out onto the pitch for 2.30pm kick-off the home team were buoyed not just by their manager's confidence, but by the unprecedented home support that greeted them. Normally for a home game, Ferranti were lucky if 200 people turned up to form what was a loyal but select crowd. Now, enticed by the prospect of an unpredictable cup tie, and with no other 'big games' in the city, the crowd had swelled to around 2,000. For the Ferranti team it was an unusual and exhilarating atmosphere. Though Elgin had brought some loyal fans, most of the crowd were cheering for the Edinburgh works side.

This unfamiliar atmosphere may, however, have been Ferranti's undoing in the early exchanges. As soon as referee Arthur McDonald – an experienced League official – blew the whistle for kick-off, Elgin's more experienced side went on the attack. The Highland team took the game by the scruff of the neck and were soon creating all the early chances. It came as no surprise to the muted home crowd when after just eleven minutes Elgin's experienced striker George Falconer opened his side's account with a header from a Gerry Graham cross; nor when Graham himself added a second barely ten minutes later. Despite the advantage of playing down the slope in the first half, Ferranti were now 2-0 down with three-quarters of the match still to play and the home fans braving this chilly January afternoon feared the worse. Were Ferranti – as some had critics had whispered before the game – simply out of their depth at this level?

The works team were swift in their reply. The emerging golden boy of the team Ian Martin made it 2-1 after 34 minutes with a stunning left-foot shot, while at the other end Graham missed a good chance to put the Highland side out of reach. Suddenly it seemed that the momentum in the game had switched. The second half was dominated by Ferranti, who were now showing the sort of form that manager John Bain had hinted at before the start of the game. They still showed fallibility at the back, but with goalie Brian Simpson on heroic form, this did not seem to matter. With twenty minutes to go another outstanding Ferranti player, winger Jim Sivewright, powered down the wing on an overlap, and his powerful shot from the edge of the area skimmed through a confusion of attackers and defenders to find the back of the net. The score guaranteed a hectic finish, with both sides having chances to win the game, as the now passionate crowd willed their side to score again. It ended in a draw with honours pretty even. Elgin's midfield star Billy Dingwall afterwards admitted they could have lost the game at the end, and were surprised by the standard of Ferranti's play. 'We thought we had them well beaten when we were two up,' he admitted. 'They came back strongly and they the game could have gone either way.'

For Ferranti, the draw may have been a disappointment after their second half display, but it was at least proof that the side was worthy of their place in the Scottish Cup and had earned the respect of even those who had been critical of their ability.

The replay was to be – perhaps inevitably – something of an anti-climax for the Edinburgh side. Having put so much effort into the dramatic game at City Park, it was always going to be hard for the Thistle side to rise to the occasion in the return match at Elgin's Borough Briggs ground a week later.

Nonetheless, manager John Bain remained determined before the game, predicting that if his side played at the top of their game, they would go through to the next round. The players, who were only on expenses, and modest ones at that, were also offered the incentive of a trip to London to watch that season's England-Scotland Home International at Wembley if they beat Elgin. As they took the long coach trip up north on Friday 19th January, the inexperienced Ferranti team was determined to make Elgin fight all the way. They were bolstered by the presence on the day of Ferranti director Sir John Toothill, who had flown up in an executive jet to watch the match.

However, in a game that had been threatened with postponement because of a frozen pitch, the Edinburgh side suffered a double blow. They lost 2-1 in a hard-fought game in which the Highland side proved just too strong. Second, and almost as bad, they lost their talented young striker Ian Martin with a broken ankle. This now threatened the side's hopes in the rest of the East of Scotland season. The outcome was undoubtedly a bitter disappointment for Ferranti. They had been tantalisingly close to going through to the Third Round of the cup, where they would have met full league opposition in the form of Hamilton Academicals. Instead they were out of the cup, facing a long trip home – and their star striker would be sidelined for weeks, if not months.

John Bain refused to be downcast by the setback, however, and was full of praise not just for his own team, but also for the hospitality of their hosts Elgin City. In one of those little stories that illustrate the true camaraderie that exists between sporting rivals, Bain revealed that when Ian Martin had broken his ankle, the Elgin chairman had himself driven the injured player to hospital for an x-ray. Then, when Martin was ready to return to the ground and link up with his teammates, the home club had laid on a taxi at their own expense. It was a generous gesture, which touched the Edinburgh side. Money – or the lack of it – was always a major consideration for clubs in those days just as much as it is today.

Not that generosity had been uppermost in the SFA's minds for this game. In a curious footnote to the match, the referee for the replay had been Nairn official Alan Gall, and not, as normal practice demanded, Arthur McDonald from Livingston, who had officiated in the first tie. McDonald said he was disappointed at this break with usual practice and in not getting the replay, while the SFA's excuse was that the travel and accommodation expenses would have been too high – a reminder that shortage of money in Scottish football administration is nothing new either. Indeed, it could be argued the desire by Scottish football authorities to save money lay behind some of changes that were now looming in the game – and that would have a huge knock-on effect on Ferranti.

For now, though chairman and manager John Bain thought little beyond the exit from the Scottish Cup and the rest of the season that lay ahead. And he was in generous mood himself towards the players, announcing that they would still enjoy their ' win bonus' of a trip to Wembley for the Home International, even though they had lost. 'They put up such a magnificent display in their first competition that we feel they deserve their weekend in London,' was the manager's verdict. Few would have disagreed with him. Though Ferranti could have beaten Elgin, there was certainly no disgrace in losing to a side whose home ground had become something of a cup fortress in recent years. Reaching the second round of the Cup, and going out only after a replay, had indeed been a solid achievement for the SFA newcomers. It was the culmination of hard work and lobbying by the club and its allies in high places to have got this far, and more cup glory was surely to come in the future. The next milestone for Ferranti could only be the altogether more daunting one of full Scottish Football League membership. Unlike entry into the SFA, however, this was not something that the great and the good of the Edinburgh works team – many of whose players still worked for the firm – were even dare considering at this stage in their history. A decent Cup run and a solid position in the East of Scotland League were the height of their ambition just for now.

In football, as in all of life, however, timing is everything. It was at this point that the politics of the national game and behind the scenes wrangles were to create major upheavals in the sport. And these changes would end up by propelling Ferranti Thistle into the centre stage of Scottish football. If this works team ever wanted to make it into the big time of the professional game, they would have to seize the unexpected opportunity that would shortly come their way.

The professional game in Scotland had been in the doldrums during the early 1970's. Attendances were falling, even at the colossi of the Scottish game, Celtic and Rangers. For example, in 1970/71 season attendances in the League – which was divided into two divisions, First and Second – had fallen by a massive 143,000 year on year, with Celtic's home crowds down by 47,000 alone. Doubtless, this was in part due to the predictability of matches at that time; after all in that season the Parkhead side were moving inexorably to their sixth straight Championship win.

But the apparent drop in interest of the Scottish public in turning up for games was blamed on more than just Celtic's near-total domination of the First Division, as it then was. The general predictability drabness of play was blamed, and the fact that so many of the best players from Scotland were heading south in ever-larger numbers to enjoy the financial trappings of the English game. Also in the firing line were the emergence of radio and television (both within and outside the game) and the increasing growth of rival forms of leisure and entertainment. At this time, television was still regarded by football officialdom as more as a threat to football than as a serious form of income. Meanwhile the slump in attendances at smaller clubs was allegedly made worse by a change in working practices. As fewer people worked on Saturday, the bigger clubs were able to take large numbers of travelling supporters with them – which meant that clubs such as Partick Thistle and Clyde were not picking up a boost in crowds when the Old Firm teams were away.

There was also thought to be a real stagnation in the two League divisions, which perhaps fed into the predictability of the football. This was partly blamed on money, or rather the lack of it. Rumours persisted of Second Division clubs who were seemingly heading for promotion and then would miss out at the last minute thanks to a mysterious late run of poor results. The theory was that gaining promotion was too expensive, taking into account extra and longer travel, greater accommodation costs, players' wages and ground standards, and that these costs would not be offset by increased revenue from bitter crowds and media money. Put bluntly, some clubs reckoned they could not afford to get promoted.

It was in such a worrying atmosphere in 1973 that Hibernian – in the form of chairman Tom Hart – and later Rangers as well, called informal meetings of leading clubs to discuss what could be done to improve the game's fortunes. These included possible changes in television contracts, a re-allocation of gate funds, and even the innovation of new end of season awards for the best player in each position. Little of substance was changed in the Annual General Meeting of League in 1973, save the rejection of a controversial plan put forward by the Management Committee to change the offside rule. (This had been tried in the Drybourgh Cup in 1973, an experiment in which the 18-yard line of the penalty area was extended to the touchlines, and that the offside rule only applied within these two areas. Critics pointed out that to adopt this proposal would put Scotland at odds with everyone else in the world and therefore handicap Scottish players during internationals.)

But the League's management committee was already working on a much more radical idea – splitting the two large divisions into three smaller ones. To overcome the problem of having a Third Division – something no League club would want to 'demoted' into – the idea was to have a First and Second Divisions as before – but with a Premier Division at the top. This would have just ten teams, who would play each other four times, with two teams relegated – to the First Division – each season. The First and Second Divisions would have fourteen teams each, who would play each other twice. The important point about this proposal – from the point of view of Ferranti Thistle and other non-League sides – was that there were currently 37 league teams; and this new structure being mooted in late 1973 and early 1974 would require 38 clubs. In other words, if this shake-up were to be approved, another club would be needed to join the Scottish Football League to make up the numbers. The question was, who?

Even at the start of 1974, when these major changes in top-flight football were in the air, it would be fair to say that possible membership of the Scottish Football League was not even close to being on the agenda at Ferranti Thistle. Aside from its playing activities, the efficient running of the team through the Recreation Club and with the backing of the company meant that the situation behind the scenes were relatively stable. It is true that money was, as ever, tight for this amateur side. In the previous season, chairman (and manager) John Bain had reckoned that the home cup match against Elgin City cost Ferranti £100 alone, once the visitor's travelling costs were taken into account. And though the electronics giant gave a great deal of moral support for the exploits of their Scottish team, they gave no actual financial backing for the side. Nor were they in a position to do so even if they had wanted to; as already mentioned, behind the scenes the company was at the time in deep financial difficulty and had no spare money to spend on footballing adventures. Yet, Bain and his fellow committee members ran the football side of Ferranti tightly and responsibly, and this meant they were never seriously over-reached financially. Despite all this, the notion of becoming a part of the most senior league in Scotland, with the extra burden of expenses and financial responsibility, as well as the potential rewards, was not a topic of conversation among the Ferranti officials, players or even their loyal supporters. Moreover, having only recently been accepted as full members of the SFA, it was reckoned to be a little premature to think about yet another big step up in status for this still young club.

The real passion at this time was generated by Thistle's on the field performances in the 1973/74 season. Though the previous season had tailed off disappointingly after the defeat by Elgin, and they had failed to win the East of Scotland League (partly due to Ian Martin's injury) they maintained their growing cup form into the next campaign. In the Scottish Qualifying Cup Ferranti showed their confidence by sweeping aside teams Threave Rovers, Burntisland Shipyard, and Edinburgh University to earn the right to face fellow Edinburgh side the Civil Service Strollers in a two-leg final. In the first game, at City Park on November 3rd, it was Ferranti who did the strolling as they comfortably outplayed the Civil Service to come out 4-0 winners. Once again, their fit again young striker Martin – who worked in the Sheet Metal department at Crewe Toll – was the hero with two of the goals. Neil Nisbet and Jimmy McArthur shared the other two. After that display, the second leg was little more than a formality, and the 2-0 Ferranti victory sealed a very handsome 6-0 aggregate to take the Cup. It was a welcome piece of silverware for the works team, a triumph that owed as much to dedication and hard work of the management team and support as it did to a talented and largely youthful group of players.

Now the club, which had already qualified for the Scottish Cup proper when they beat Burntisland, aimed to go one step better than the previous land and at least reach the third round of the competition, the point at which the big boys from the First and Second Division joined in. Their path was smoothed by a first round bye, and Ferranti were pleased when news through of their Second Round opponents – Civil Service Strollers, the team they had already dispatched in the Qualifying Cup. For the third time that season, Ferranti overcame their Edinburgh rivals, moving the club once more into un-chartered territory, the third round of the Scottish Cup. Before the draw, manager John Bain said he hoped to meet 'any First Division team, away from home' and he got his wish. Ferranti were drawn to play First Division Partick Thistle at their Firhill ground. Partick may have not been the most glamorous Glasgow side in the competition, but they were no mugs either, and clearly played at a level far higher than anything Ferranti had yet encountered. The idea of leaving the comfort of their own, sloping pitch to take on a First Division side – and one who had recently beaten Hibernian and drawn with Rangers at Ibrox – filled some Ferranti supporters with dread as well as excitement.

Yet once again, the club was determined not be overawed. The coaches Lawrie Glasson and Walter Hay – another Ferranti veteran – drove the players hard in extra training sessions and the team responded well. Even the problems of the energy crisis hitting the Western world at the time were turned to the club's advantage. Though the restriction on using floodlights hampered evening training sessions, the three-day working week imposed by the energy restrictions at least meant that the part-timers could train together during the daytime.

Meanwhile manager John Bain was publicly defiant about his team's chances. 'We don't mind being called "rabbits" as long as people don't think we are a pushover. We know what we'll face at Firhill, but there is every confidence among the players that we can stretch Thistle. They'll be faster than us. But if we can contain their opening burst we could catch them on the break. Smaller clubs from England have already caused shocks – and we can do the same.'

Much of Ferranti's confidence came from the performance of their defence, which had tightened up since last season. Their new goalie Derek Gray, who had been with Stirling Albion, had kept ten clean sheets in the last 13 games, though he had been beaten in their last match, against Hawick Royal Albert (who beat Ferranti twice that season). In front of Gray, the defence of Allan McDonald, Allan Robertson, Neil Nesbit and Denis McGurk was tough and well-organised, well-led by the experienced Robertson. Up front, meanwhile, Ian Martin was still the main danger man. Their cup record that season looked impressive on paper too; so far they had scored 13 goals in the Qualifying and Scottish Cup, and conceded just two.

Once again, the telegrams flooded in from various parts of the Ferranti Empire, those overseas as well as in England, in the build-up to the fixture, which was to be played on Sunday 27 January 1974. The director and former general manager of the Scottish arm of Ferranti Sir John Toothill was unable to attend this match but wished the side well for the game. The firm's insurance manager Harry Wolfenden, based in Manchester, cheekily sent a telegram assuring the team that 'arrangements have been made to insure the Cup'.

The club itself guaranteed that it would have decent support over in Glasgow by offering to pay the admission ticket for any fan who contributed just 50 pence towards the cost of the bus trip. This ploy from the Recreation Club ensured some six coach loads of supporters made the journey from the capital.

After their mini cup run last season in their first time in the Scottish Cup, the 1,000 –1 outsiders Ferranti were once again capturing the imagination of the football public both in Scotland and further afield; the word 'fairytale' was now often used in the newspapers to describe the little club and its achievements.

When Sunday came, however, the fairytale – at least for this season – came to an abrupt end. It may have had something to do with the powerful atmosphere created by the crowd of 6,000 that turned up to watch the game – comfortably the largest Ferranti had experienced – but whatever the reason the East of Scotland League side were on the wrong end of a stinging 6-1 defeat. The works side had shown glimpses of their ability and were determined to attack at every opportunity, deploying both their wingers Crawford and Sivewright and were warmly applauded by the enthusiastic and sympathetic crowd. But in the end they were overwhelmed by the superior power, organisation, and skill of their First Division hosts. This was typified by the 'Jags' skipper Ronnie Glavin who registered a hat-trick, including the opening goal after 22 minutes. For Ferranti, right-winger Charlie Crawford scored a consolation goal with a rare header in the 76th minute, following a cross by substitute Brock. Afterwards, the media were kind about their performance, and pointed out that the final score was a little harsh on the Edinburgh outfit. 'It was not as easy as the scoreline suggests,' said the man from the *Scottish Daily Express*. 'Ferranti.... thoroughly deserved their standing ovation at the end.' Elsewhere, the Glasgow-based *Herald* wrote of the side's 'enormous heart and neat skills' while the Edinburgh-based *Scotsman* applauded the team's 'splendid display'. It would be churlish to regard these last remarks as patronising; it was indeed the view of many who watched that match that the smaller Thistle side were beaten but not disgraced in their performance. Once again, it was left to the manager to put a brave face on the outcome. John Bain suggested the team had won some 'new friends' with their display. 'Our lads appreciated the large support we had, and rose to the occasion. The result could have been closer but I'm afraid Partick's full-time training told in the end.'

Bain also hinted at the impact the game could have on recruiting new players to the club, especially from inside the company. 'I now hope we can encourage more Ferranti players to join us,' he remarked.

There was also the bonus of having a £500 cheque as their share of gate receipts, a significant sum for such a club. All in all it was felt that the experience had been a good one, despite the size of the defeat, and that Ferranti could look forward to even better things in the future. Meanwhile Bain said that by way of reward he and the committee were pledging 'something special' for the players at the end of the season. The manager had no way of knowing that this promise was to come true in a wholly unexpected and unplanned way.

Their two cup runs, and the fact that they could be portrayed as a lowly works team taking on the big teams of Scottish football, had guaranteed Ferranti Thistle a much higher profile than many other non-league clubs. Already the side was beginning to build a small but highly motivated fan base outside of Scotland. Yet when it came to the planned reorganisation of Scottish football, Ferranti's name was on practically no one's lips – including Ferranti officials themselves. As winter gave way to spring in 1974, the Management Committee of the Football League were far advanced in their plans for a three-division system, with a Premier Division followed by a First and Second. This still needed approval by the member clubs, but it was felt that Scottish football needed change and a shake-up, and the measure was expected to be passed. It was not lost on a number of ambitious non-league clubs, therefore, that the potential requirement for a 38th member of the League to complete the new division structure was fast becoming a certainty. In late March and early April, intense lobbying was under way by the interested clubs. Top of the list of those determined to press for League status were the larger clubs of the Highland League, and especially Elgin City – Ferranti's old cup rivals – Inverness Thistle and Ross County. In footballing terms, they had a good case, and it was widely reckoned they could probably more than hold their own in the lower reaches of the Second Division at the very least. The problem, as ever with clubs from that league, was the distance and weather. For impoverished Second Division Clubs, the long drive up north meant greater travel costs, expensive overnight accommodation, plus the possibility that games could be postponed at short notice because of harsher weather conditions. The northern clubs understandably felt aggrieved that these non-football arguments always came up at such times; yet with the professional game in Scotland already suffering financial problems it seemed unlikely that many Second Division clubs would vote for anything that could make their financial predicament even worse. According to observers at the time, this concern over transport issues was pressed hard by, among others, the late Tom Fagan of Albion Rovers. Fagan was said to 'shudder' at the very idea of travelling to what he (and some others) considered to be the 'frozen north'. He also pointed that any of his players – who were part-timers – worked in the local economy of Airdrie and Coatbridge; they could simply not afford to take time off to play in mid-week games.

Another, bolder idea, was that the 38th club could be from England. Both South Shield and especially Gateshead were certainly keen to discuss joining the Scottish set-up. These north-east England clubs suffered from some of the same geographical problems as the High League outfits. They were a long way from many other English clubs – travelling to Plymouth, Torquay or Bournemouth would be a major logistical exercise. Many of the Scottish clubs were far closer, easily accessible by rail for example, and in addition, an English club could perhaps bring in a whole new audience (and thus money) into the Scottish game. The drawback was the obvious one – how could you have such an obviously English club in the Scottish

League? (Berwick Rangers, coming from the English border town is clearly an exception to this rule, having played in the Scottish League for many years.)

Another club mentioned as a possible candidate for membership was Hawick Royal Albert. On the playing side, Hawick were certainly the match of sides such as Ferranti, whom they had beaten twice that season in the East Scotland League already. The argument against them was as a Borders team, they came from more of a rugby than a football area; though why this was not seen as a golden opportunity to encourage more football support in that area is unclear.

These, then, were the names that were being mentioned as likely candidates to be the 38th club. Up till now, no one had mentioned Ferranti Thistle as a possible League member, and there was a very good reason for this – no one at Ferranti had apparently considered it. Though the club and its officials did have ambitions in that direction one day, it was – as discussed earlier – felt that this was still too early in the club's development. It was, after all, only two years before that the club had become full members of the SFA and thus eligible for the Scottish Cup. And it was only five years since the works team had been playing on their convenient but windswept works recreation pitch at Crewe Toll. Could they really be ready for League status so soon?

If the officials at Ferranti hesitated at the prospect of this elevation, one man did not. The sports editor of the *Evening News* in Edinburgh, the late Stewart Brown, wrote an article on 2 April 1974 in which he discussed the forthcoming reorganisation, and mulled dispassionately over the likely candidates. He quickly ruled out the likely prospects of the Highland and English clubs, and was doubtful too about the football credentials of rugby-mad Hawick. But what about, suggested Brown, another name altogether – Ferranti Thistle?

The advantages of a Ferranti bid were obvious. They were centrally placed, which would avoid long travelling for most likely opponents. Brown also argued that the club had 'reasonable facilities' at their Corporation-owned ground at City Park, and that they could have the backing of the electronics company whose name they already bore. Brown wrote by way of comparison: 'I can think of no better example than the Dutch club, PSV Eindhoven, who have the financial help of Phillips behind them all the way. This firm has poured thousands of guilders into the club and the pay-off could come soon since PSV are level in the championship with Feyenoord and one point behind Ajax.' Brown went

31

on: 'I'm not suggesting that Ferranti would support their works team to the same extent, but they have the resources to put the club on a sound footing if they attempted to achieve League status.'

In preparing his article, Brown had approached the Ferranti club chairman and manager John Bain for his views on the subject. Bain confessed the club had not even considered the matter and was decidedly lukewarm about the idea – but was nonetheless careful not to rule it out. His comments were: 'We haven't discussed it and I doubt whether our support would justify it with running costs much higher than they are at the moment. But it might work if we were allowed to play on a Sunday when Hibs and Hearts stick rigidly to Saturdays.'

These seemed the words of a man who had just seen the germ of an idea, and now wanted to see if it could work.

The *Evening News* article undoubtedly kick-started Ferranti's interest in joining the League. It was already clear that re-organisation of the League divisions into three *would* be happening in time for the 1975/76 season, and so the only issue now seemed to be who the 38th club would be. The Leagues AGM was scheduled for 24 May so there was little time to lose if Ferranti were to go ahead and make a formal application to join the League.

The next few days at Ferranti were taken up with lengthy and sometimes awkward discussions between the club officials and those from the company about any possible aid for the club and any application. Leading the case for seeking League membership were Bain himself and Bill Mill, club secretary and one of the stalwarts of Ferranti football. They saw quickly that while this chance had come early – perhaps a little too early – opportunities to join the League did not come often. If they turned their back on this chance, they might have to wait a very long time before another opportunity presented itself to join the League set up.

The company wanted to be helpful – there was genuine affection for the team and pride over the success of the club – but there was a problem. The company was in financial problems, even though this was a closely guarded secret and not revealed even to trusted and senior staff such as John Bain. Could they really justify offering backing to a football team?

In the end the persuasions of Bain and Mill won the day, with the company offering full support and accepting that it could gain something from the very obvious association with a League football club. So it was that within days of the *Evening News* floating the idea, John Bain was able to announce in the same publication that they had indeed applied to the

Scottish Football League for membership.

Bain told Stewart Brown: 'The company have promised to finance us all the way and now we're going all out to win support from other clubs before the annual meeting of the League.'

He then set out why Ferranti thought they had a good chance of success. 'We believe that geographically the inclusion of Ferranti would be more acceptable to other clubs than any team from the Highland League of one from the North of England. Maybe our visitors would receive no more than the guarantee [this was the minimum money an away side was guaranteed to collect from the fixture], but their expenses would be much less too.'

It was the opening salvo in Ferranti's brief but determined campaign. Though they had openly conceded their gate receipts might not match those of a club such as Elgin City, they had cunningly raised the perennial and thorny issue of travel costs. This was a handy carrot to dangle in front of wavering lower division clubs. It would be fair to say that Ferranti's campaign was based as much on what or where they were not – not in the Highlands, not in England, not in a rugby area – as on what or where they *were*. There were in this sense the ultimate compromise candidate – the option most acceptable (or least unacceptable) to a broad range of other clubs.

The rival applicants, especially those in the Highland League, were understandably dismayed that Ferranti were now going for League membership. Many of them had been around much longer than this obscure works team and had better and more consistent playing records over the years. For them, this had all the hallmarks of yet another Central belt stitch-up from clubs who were unwilling to travel too far – and against opposition who might well beat them. Surely a Ferranti fixture would just be easy points (and thus pools money) for the existing league members; and weren't the works team being bankrolled by a giant company as well? That, in any case, was some of the thoughts of the Highland clubs as Thistle officials began their charm offensive on the other 37 league clubs. Much of this was done privately, with Bain and Mill talking to a wide range of officials at other clubs to press their claims. They had already shown they had close links with and the support of the big two Edinburgh clubs, Hearts and Hibs and good links with Celtic too. It was not long, in fact, before the press coverage completely changed tone – in many observers' eyes Ferranti Thistle had now overtaken Inverness Thistle become the favourites to gain League membership.

The growing mood of optimism was reflected in John Bain's public as well as his private comments. One the eve of the May 24 AGM Bain told journalists: 'I'm biased of course, but I think we must have an excellent chance. Like all the other clubs applying for the vacant place, we've been doing a lot of lobbying – and the signs are very favourable. Quite a number of clubs have promised us their support.'

Just how many clubs would do so emerged the next day at this most tense of League AGM's. Inverness, too, had been intense in their lobbying, and were determined that mere geography would not defeat their case.

The result of the first ballot, when it came, was a cliffhanger. The two leading candidates by far were the two Thistles – Inverness and Ferranti. They had tied on 13 votes each. The two clubs then had to go into a second ballot to determine the outright winner; and the result, though still close, was a clear win for Ferranti by 21-16. The outcome, when it was known, caused considerable recriminations, not least among the Highland teams.

Had just one of the other Highland applicants dropped out, then Inverness Thistle might have won on the first ballot. The result was inevitably seen as the Central Belt fix they had warned about, an accusation made stronger still by developments that were soon to follow.

For Ferranti, of course, it was a moment of excitement and elation, if perhaps tinged with a slight apprehension about just what lay in store for the club. John Bain spoke delightedly of the great challenge, and promised the club would work hard to earn their place – while also striking that note of caution. 'We are deadly serious. But there is a lot of work to be done.'

Scottish Works Manager of the company Tom Neal was equally pleased but hinted the firm might not be the financial backers that many outsiders at least had assumed. He told the works newspaper *Ferranti News*: 'We anticipate the team will get tremendous support, both morally and financially, from all our employees – and there are over five thousand in Scotland.'

It was an apparent attempt to put the onus of support on the staff at Ferranti rather than on the firm's own coffers.

This situation is best explained by recent observations made by Sir Donald McCallum, General Manager of Ferranti in Scotland until 1985, who told the author: 'There were complaints from some of the existing members [of the League] about this new team backed by the finances of this electronics giant. Little did they know that the company was in deep financial trouble at that time? I found it very ironic but of course one could say nothing.'

The financial backing of the club by its parent company was in fact to be far less than anyone could have supposed at the time, and for a far shorter period. But such matters were for the future. What did seem clear in May 1974 was that a club bearing the Ferranti name and playing at City Park – the old League home of Edinburgh City – would be joining the old Second Division for the 1974/75 season as the League prepared for re-organisation.

Within days of the controversial vote to admit Ferranti as an associate League member, however, even these two certainties had to be questioned. During discussions in early June between the club, the firm and league officials it became clear that the League wanted certain changes and assurances. These issues came to a head at a meeting between Ferranti club and firm representatives and members of the Management Committee of the League. There were now, it appeared, two conditions that had to be met before Ferranti could join the League. The first was that the club had to change its name. Second, the team's home ground at City Park was deemed to be unfit, and the club would have to move to another Corporation-owned pitch – Meadowbank Stadium.

Both ultimatums dropped like bombshells on Ferranti, a shock both to club and company alike. The questions came thick and fast. Without its name on the club, why would Ferranti want to help it financially, even supposing it could? What would be left of a club that had been based firmly on the Ferranti Recreation Club at Crewe Toll if one severed all links with the Ferranti name? And could the club really flourish in a large but soulless venue such as the Meadowbank Stadium that had been built for Edinburgh to stage the 1970 Commonwealth games? Moreover, what would Highland League teams make of the fact that the very team that had been voted into the League over their heads did not even meet basic requirements for entry? Finally, were these drastic steps really worth taking in view of the expected financial struggle that lay ahead in the world of league football?

The initial response both of team officials John Bain and Will Mill and the company was that the Ferranti name should continue and that they also stay at City Park. So, at the end of June, they lodged an appeal. The management Committee of the League considered the appeal on 2 July, but the message that came back was adamant. League Secretary Thomas Maule wrote bluntly to John Bain on 3 July: 'The Management Committee decided that the two conditions laid down...must be complied with.'

And nor could the Committee wait for long for an answer. 'I have also been instructed to inform you that your club must convey your decision to me not later than 10th July 1974,' wrote Mr Maule.

The Ferranti club was in a terrible dilemma. Here, in their grasp, was the culmination of many years hard work, a rare and possibly unique chance to join the Football League; for many at the club the ultimate dream of any footballer. Yet to achieve that dream, they would have to sacrifice their name, part of their heritage, and their ground. Still, the decision had to be made, and made quickly – within a week. With heavy hearts it was made. The club would accept League membership. Ferranti, the works team from Edinburgh that had started playing against pub teams, had finally made it into the big time. But they had done so at a terrible cost. They may have become the newest members of the Scottish Football League, yet just at this moment, they didn't even have a name. The ensuing row over the name was to blight what should have been the proudest period in the club's brief history.

3

A Tough Baptism

ONE OF THE MOST DIFFICULT experiences any football team can endure is changing its name. A club can swap managers, get rid of most of its players, lose the chairman and even move grounds, and the supporters will still readily identify with it. Yet change the name of the club, and something dies in a fan's heart, even if they are able to change their allegiance to the newly-named side. There can of course be reasons why a club might chose to change its name – as of course the later history of Ferranti so controversially demonstrates. For example, a club may move to a new catchment area and want to change its name to identify with its new host audience (as was to happen to the club in 1995). But the situation facing Ferranti Thistle in June 1974 was something even worse, and more painful; they were being *ordered* by the Scottish Football League to change their name.

The League's position had become quite clear in June 1974. Ferranti Thistle had to meet the two conditions the League's management committee were laying down, or their proposed entry to the Second Division for the 1974/75 season would be blocked. The two conditions were, as we have seen, that the club lost the 'Ferranti' part of its name and that the club (whatever it was going to be called) had to move from City Park to the large, cavernous Meadowbank Stadium.

The stipulation over Thistle's change of venue was understandable and perhaps inevitable. The standard of facilities at their Pilton ground were not high to begin with; and without new money to spend on them had become further run down. For a small club such as Ferranti the repair bill that would be needed to bring it up immediately to the right standards – even the relatively modest ones of the Second Division – would have been crippling. Nonetheless Ferranti had initially hoped to stay at City Park, at least for a season. They had even opened discussions with the ground's owners Edinburgh Parks Department about reducing the number of junior matches played there, in an attempt to ensure the playing surface stayed in good condition for League football.

However, once it was decided that Ferranti would enter the Second Division immediately in time for the 1974/75 season – and ahead of the re-structuring of the divisions in 1975/76 – then a change of ground became a near-certainty.

The change of name, however, was a different matter altogether. The issue soon overshadowed what should have been an exciting summer as the club prepared for the ultimate challenge of League football.

Though Ferranti had suggested in their initial application to the Football League that they might be willing to consider changing their name if that was required, club officials were surprised and hurt with the vehemence with which this was imposed upon them. The club had hoped that if a change was necessary they could reach an amicable compromise over the new title. After all, Ferranti Thistle had been their name since the club's formation after the end of the war, and certainly since it had joined the East of Scotland League in 1953. The name had a history, a meaning and an identity – surely this could not be abandoned lightly? So why did it have to change?

The League (and indeed the Scottish Football association as well) took a very different view of history and tradition. After all, how could the Scottish Football League possibly consider allowing a club into its ranks that was named after a commercial enterprise – a company? This, surely, was commercialism and sponsorship at its most naked, complained the grandees of the Scottish football establishment. The club would have to compete with a new name – and one that did not involve Ferranti in any way.

Even at the time there were plenty of commentators and newspapers columnists who could not understand the reasoning of the League. Ferranti, after all, were joining a professional league, in which players (many of them) got paid, and in a world in which companies sponsored football competitions such as the Texaco Cup. Meanwhile clubs received money from adverts placed in programmes or on boards at grounds. Surely commerce was at the very heart of the modern game?

Writing in Edinburgh's *Evening News*, George Harkness reflected the views of many in his opposition to the enforced name change, and criticised the lack of logic behind the ultimatum. 'I see no reason why Thistle should have to change their name,' he wrote. 'They have played under the Ferranti banner for 20 years now and, in the past two seasons, the SFA accepted them as qualifiers for the Scottish Cup without the least quibble.'

Another newspaper correspondent wrote at the time: '.....as a matter of hard fact the team is run as part of the welfare activities of a world-famous company which does not need to advertise its products.'

If it looked a curious decision then, it looks even more regrettable and more wrong-headed with hindsight. After all, Ferranti Thistle had grown naturally and gradually out of a factory side much as, say, Arsenal had done down in London many eyars before. To ban the Ferranti name from the club after all those years appears now to have been little more than an act of cultural vandalism inflicted on the sport by the football authorities; mingled perhaps with a touch of misguided snobbery against vulgar 'commerce'. As most fans would agree, tradition is an important part of any sport, football included, and should not be thrown away lightly.

It is possible that the ultimatum thrown down by the management committee – who incidentally claimed they were merely dotting the i's and crossing the t's of the AGM's decision – was based on a fundamental misunderstanding of the difference between Ferranti as a company and as a football club. As we have already seen, the company was in a poor financial state, even if no one outside a few senior executives knew this at the time. There was very little slack to be spent on the relative luxury of a football team, no matter what the benefits of the publicity might be. In any case the electronics giant had never really regarded their football team in Scotland as part of a serious marketing strategy. Yes, there was corporate pride at the side's achievements, of course, and senior executives such as John Toothill in particular had always taken a keen personal interest in the team and when necessary had backed this up with support. But for the company, the unprecedented success of the football team was a happy accident, not a marketing ploy. The club had arisen organically from the ranks of enthusiastic staff at Ferranti who shared a deep passion for the game. Over the years success had built on success, as each generation of player sought to emulate or outdo the performances of their predecessors. In particular success had been due to a core of dedicated football enthusiasts – starting with Derek Read and Tommy Learmouth – who were also skilled players, managers and administrators who helped develop Thistle from its earliest days. By 1974, John Bain had been manager of the club for 20 years, providing virtually unprecedented continuity, as well as being a full-time member of staff – a shop floor supervisor – at the Ferranti company. Club secretary Bill Mill was another who had been with the club for years, combining playing and administration with the demands of his job as a draughtsman.

Therefore Ferranti were not seeking to force some new form of commercialism on the Football League; rather they were the incidental beneficiaries of the football skills of the company' staff. Ferranti Thistle were called Ferranti simply because that was where the club's players had come from, not from any motives of sponsorship. (Indeed Sir Donald McCallum, the general manager, has recently 'confessed' to the author that while he wished the team well, football was 'not really my game' and revealed he had rarely watched them play!).

It does appear, however, that the Football League viewed the Ferranti name with deep suspicion, as if the name alone implied some new and unwelcome commercial strategy, rather than it being simply a quirk of Scottish football history.

There were at the time bizarre rumours that the organisers of the pools promotions were behind the Scottish League's unkind verdict on Ferranti's name, though quite why this would have been the case remains unclear. The League's secretary Tommy Maule quickly dismissed the reports, though in a revealing choice of words he made it clear that it was the management committee who were behind name change ruling, and not the wider club membership. He told reporters: 'The 37 clubs voted Ferranti into the League and left the cleaning up work to the management committee. It was their decision to make Ferranti change their name.'

In any case, and whatever their real motives and reasoning for this 'cleaning up work', the League was adamant that the name 'Ferranti' had to be removed entirely from the ranks of professional football in Scotland. Even the apparently obvious and reasonable compromises were rejected. For example 'Edinburgh Ferranti' was quickly dismissed, as was the even more reasonable abbreviated version, Edinburgh FFC. That was apparently an 'F' too far for the nervous officials who inhabited 188 West Regent Street in Glasgow, home of the Scottish Football League.

So, if Edinburgh Ferranti was deemed too dangerous, and even Edinburgh FFC was ruled to be beyond the bounds of footballing decency, then what could this new League club be called?

The media and public opinion were quick to get involved in this debate. In the *Evening News* George Harkness invited readers to come up with their own suggestions for the club. These suggestions ranged from the sensible to the curious and even the downright bizarre. Some played on the theme of the company and its products and technical expertise, for example Edinburgh Gyro, Gyro Thistle, Edinburgh Dynamo and Edinburgh Pathfinders. Another idea was that the club should be named after the city's most famous natural feature and be called simply Edinburgh Castle FC; while one reader thought that the city's railway station could inspire the name Edinburgh Waverly Thistle. A more linguistically-derived choice was Edinburgh Dunedin, using the old Gaelic name for the city, while another fan wanted the name Edinburgh Emmet after a former local team that had played at Bathgate Park, and yet another favoured simply Ferry Thistle.

Perhaps the most enticing name was the one suggested by a woman reader Patricia Cockburn from Wester Hailes. She suggested the picturesque name Edinburgh Citadel. Mrs Cockburn wrote: 'Do we not possess a famous citadel in Edinburgh? Of course we do! There is the castle, perched high on a rock, and very dear to the Scottish heart. It is indeed a citadel and in days of old our invading enemies could not scale the steep rock.' The name conjured up an impressive image for a sporting team. Sadly it was never taken up.

Though the press and public understandably saw the amusing side of the name controversy – as well as appreciating the more serious aspects – it was of course never laughing matter for the club officials at Ferranti. They were just a few weeks from the start of a new season, in a new league and a new stadium, and here they were; still with no name.

As time ran out, manager John Bain cancelled his family's annual holiday to Kent to stay and grapple with the crisis, no small sacrifice in an era when lengthy vacation breaks were usually taken at fixed times or not at all.

Like the readers of the *Evening News*, Ferranti too were mulling over various possibilities. Bain revealed that they had been thinking of the name Edinburgh Thistle, which at least had the advantage of maintaining part of the club's old name. Unfortunately for them, however, the name was already registered as a football club with the Scottish Football Association. A similar objection faced the straightforward choice of Edinburgh City. That had been the name of Ferranti's predecessors at City Park. Founded in 1928, City had been elected to the Second Division in 1931. Though they were later to disband as a football team, their popular and recreational City Club kept going (and still does). More pertinently, the name of the club was still registered with the SFA. (Edinburgh City reformed as a team in 1986 and are in the East of Scotland League – and by an interesting twist of fate they now occupy the Meadowbank Stadium.) One London-based fan who had apparently had connections with the old Edinburgh City was so excited at the prospect of the club name being revised as a Scottish league team, that he offered Ferranti the sum of £10 towards club funds if they adopted that name. But it was not to be.

Another possibility discussed was Crewe Thistle, in honour of the site of the main Ferranti factory in Edinburgh, which was sited at Crewe Toll. But it emerged that even this name had been registered elsewhere, by a non-league side in the English town of Crewe. Other possibilities that were seriously mooted – and here perhaps was a sign of increasing desperation over the issue – were those of Edina Thistle and even Third Lanark. Lanark had been the last club to leave the Scottish League.

Tracing the exact origins of the choice of Meadowbank Thistle for the new league club is not easy. It is far easier to see *how* the name came about and why they were compelled to use the name Meadowbank. By now, in July 1974, the unnamed club was all set for the move to the Commonwealth stadium, the ground change proving to be the least traumatic of the two conditions of League membership that had been imposed on them. Incorporating the name Meadowbank had a certain logic to it, as it would help to locate the club in a geographical area. At the same time, keeping Thistle would be some small reminder of the club's previous incarnation. The initial idea seems to have been that the club should be called Edinburgh Meadowbank, and this seemed to strike a chord with at least some in the club. John Bain told sports writer George Harkness in the Evening News: 'One suggestion I did like came from a councillor who thought we should call ourselves Edinburgh Meadowbank, but that is a matter which would have to come under discussion.'

Indeed, behind the scenes the ultimate owners of the stadium, the city council, were suggesting that incorporating the name 'Meadowbank' into the club was more than just an idea. It has since emerged that the council made the club's adoption of the name their one overriding condition on its use of the stadium. After the construction of the stadium for the Commonwealth games, the council was keen to justify the cost of the building by finding another high profile and this time permanent use for the arena. What better than a League football club – and using the stadium's name?

Initially, however, Bain and other committee members at Ferranti favoured using Edinburgh in the name. This reflected their position as the new third League club of the capital behind Hearts and Hibernian.

As July passed by, time was running out for the officials to make a decision. The three most popular words to include in the name were, it seems, Meadowbank, Thistle and Edinburgh. Clearly one of them would have to go, unless the club was to be lumbered with an unwieldy name, and Meadowbank had already been stipulated by the council. Eventually the Ferranti team committee came to vote on the choice. The arguments ranged too and fro, but eventually the outcome was clear. From now on, Ferranti Thistle would be known as Meadowbank Thistle. Though not everyone associated with Ferranti was overjoyed at this choice, it at least had the merits of being fresh and distinctive. The name had some history too, it seems. Local councillor George Theurer revealed that at the end of the First World War, when he was just 14, he had played for a team called Meadowbank Thistle. What was more, the junior team had played on an empty patch of ground where the Meadowbank Stadium now stood. Councillor Theurer described to reporters how he had become involved with the 'old' Meadowbank Thistle. ' I was living in the area and became interested in the team. I was made the hamper boy [a job involving carrying team kit and equipment around] and when they were a man short I got a game – usually at right half. The team's colours were blue with white pants.'

Having been forced to shed of a little piece of their Ferranti history, at least it seemed the new Meadowbank Thistle now had a new slice of tradition of its own to savour.

The belated decision to choose Meadowbank as a name came just in time to save the club's entry into Second Division football. There had been a real danger that the League would lose patience and postpone the side's move into the professional game. Behind the scenes, Ferranti officials were thoroughly fed up with what they saw as the high-handed way they had been dealt with by the league bureaucrats. There were even media reports that some at Ferranti now wished they had not been admitted into the League in the first place, and were regretting their application. This was not quite true – but there was great irritation at their treatment.

Publicly, club officials such as Hugh Cowan, John Bain and Bill Mill maintained a stoical stance, refusing to be critical of the League, and expressing determination that all would be well with the club. This approach was typified by Bain's comments to sports journalist George Harkness at the start of the name row when the Ferranti name was still being debated. 'There's a lot of sentiment involved,' Bain conceded. 'A lot of people have put a tremendous amount of work into the club over the years and I would feel sorry for them if the name Ferranti Thistle had to be scrapped. But we have no intention of quitting and reapplying for a place in the East of Scotland League.'

One of the worst headaches for Bain as manager was that until the name crisis was resolved he could not sign up players for the new season, which was now just a few weeks away. To offer a contract for a player, the club had to be able to puts its name at the top of the contract. As Bain pointed out, it was asking a lot of any player to expect him to sign a piece of paper with a blank space where the name of the club should be.

This meant that when the name issue was resolved and players could be signed, Bain and his colleagues had very little time to scout around for new talent. Instead, the lack of time for recruitment meant that Meadowbank chose to rely largely on the same group of players who had served them well enough in the East of Scotland League and Scottish Qualifying Cup. Events later in the coming season would show the weakness of this decision; a decision which involved an element of sentiment and an understandable sense of loyalty to players who could now achieve their dream of playing in the Football League. In the circumstances of that difficult summer for Ferranti, perhaps the club's management had little choice.

The club in any case had matters even closer to home to confront. Meadowbank Thistle needed to be put on a proper footing both financially and administratively. Thistle had always been canny with their finances over the years, a tribute to the efficiency of men such as secretary Will Mill, vice-chairman Hugh Cowan and Bain himself. However, the advent of professionalism, the resulting public gaze, the extra financial burdens, and the need for accountability meant that new systems had to be established. Administratively, the quartet of the new chairman John Blacklaw, Mill, Cowan and Bain – the so-called 'gang of Four' – were effectively to run the club side, with Bain taking prime responsibility for the playing side. He in turn was to be aided by coach Lawrie Glasson, a veteran of the side that lifted the East of Scotland Qualifying Cup in 1962/63. The officials had worked well together in the days of the East of Scotland League, though time would tell if the strains of the Second Division would take their toll on the relationships between these men.

Financially, the club hit upon the idea of setting up a Founder's Club. This attracted a total of some 180 members, each paying £1 a month to help bankroll the club. In addition, employees at Ferranti who still wanted to support the team despite its name change – and there were many – were able to contribute five pence a week from their pay packet towards the club. This was one positive contribution that the Ferranti company was able to make to the team, by allowing its payroll computer system to be used to deduct funds from participating staff. The other contribution was loan capital. If Meadowbank Thistle had any chance of survival in the league, they needed at least some capital behind them to fund any necessary purchase of kit or other equipment, and to cover travel costs at the start of the season. John Blacklaw, himself a senior executive at the company, helped negotiate a £1,000 loan from Ferranti to cover these essential start-up costs.

In the circumstances – having had their name stripped from the football team – the club's generosity with its time and money was impressive. They also had to factor in the loss of working time from Will Mill and John Bain especially, both salaried employees of the company. They were indeed magnanimous gestures, which contrasted quite sharply at the time with the rather petty-minded obsession of the League officials.

If the structure of the club was in remarkably robust shape considering the events of the summer, Meadowbank were seemingly unable to escape bad news on other fronts. One of the worst blows was the news that the Scottish Football Association – official custodians of the Scottish Cup – were insisting that the club would have to take part in the Scottish Qualifying Cup for the new season, despite Thistle's impending new League status. League teams were exempt from qualifying and started off in the full Scottish Cup. The SFA's reasoning was based on Ferranti's initial reluctance to change their name, and its decision came before the club finally changed its name to Meadowbank Thistle. It was clear that the hostility towards the Ferranti heritage was every bit as strong at the SFA as it was among League officials. The SFA President Rankin Grimshaw said publicly: 'We [have] heard Ferranti don't wish to change a name that smacks of sponsorship. So, as far as we are concerned, they cannot be members of the League and must qualify for entry into the Scottish Cup.'

As far as the Ferranti club was itself concerned, this uncompromising stance by the SFA was even more objectionable than the League's intransigence over the name change. As the SFA made its ruling, Ferranti were still in the process of negotiating with the League about their name. Indeed, John Bain already had cancelled his holiday to help deal with the crisis. The SFA's decision to force the as yet unnamed club to enter the Qualifying Cup was therefore seen by Ferranti club officials as a premature and needlessly antagonistic gesture. It reinforced the growing feeling among some at the club that ever since the League's AGM that voted them into the Second Division, the factory-based team had become increasingly isolated and friendless in the football world.

Soon, indeed, the anger at Ferranti – now Meadowbank – boiled over into outright rejection of the SFA's decision. The club decided that if it was not allowed into the Scottish Cup draw from the start, then it would withdraw from the Qualifying Cup. The club suggested that it was being treated as second class citizens, and made it clear it was no longer willing to be pushed around by bureaucrats. Manager Bain told Jim McLean of the *Scottish Daily Express*: 'this was not an easy decision to take, but we feel we should not be asked to play in the Qualifying Cup. We won't play in the tournament on the SFA's terms. We feel we shouldn't be treated any different from the rest of the clubs in the Second Division.'

He continued: 'The Scottish Cup is one of the season's major highlights. Our withdrawal would obviously be a big blow to us financially and otherwise, but we feel it was a decision taken in the best interests for the future of the club. It would be madness for us to go into the qualifying competition as our main target is to do well in the Second Division.' He predicted that playing in the competition would lead to 'fixture chaos' which in turn would place an extra burden on a club at a time when it already had quite enough new challenges to confront.

This reaction by someone such as John Bain, who was not naturally a person to seek confrontation, underlined the anger felt by the club at this time. In the space of just two months the sense of euphoria at being voted into the League had quickly dissipated, and instead been replaced by a growing feeling of frustration.

Yet the SFA refused to budge on the matter, despite Meadowbank's threat of withdrawal. The explanation provided for this by the SFA gives a good insight into how such bureaucracies function. Assistant secretary Ernie Walker said that at the time of their last meeting of the Council, Ferranti had yet not been accepted as members of the Scottish League and that therefore they had to be treated as 'ordinary non-League members of the SFA' and thus included in the Qualifying Cup. In other words, though they must have been aware that Ferranti were *going to* join the League in the near future – what after all was the purpose of the League's AGM vote in May if not that? – at the precise moment of their meeting this has not *yet* happened. Therefore it could not be taken into account. It was little wonder that the new club felt frustrated at such absurd behaviour. The new boys at Meadowbank Thistle were getting an early lesson in the vagaries of football administration.

Not only did the SFA not change its ruling – even when Meadowbank were formally accepted as members of the League – but it also warned of the dire consequences should they carry out their threat to boycott the qualifying event. 'No club can scratch just because they feel like it,' explained Ernie Walker. 'Satisfactory reasons must be given and the SFA must give consent for a team to withdraw. A team that withdraws for two years in succession loses SFA membership.'

In the end, perhaps inevitably, Meadowbank gave way and acceded to the SFA's wishes. However unreasonable the association's demands might be, the new arrivals in Scottish football could hardly afford to start a war over the Cup when all their energies had to be focussed on the League. There was criticism enough flying around. The Highland clubs, those who had watched as this upstart team from Edinburgh snatch away the prize of League membership from under their noses, were now watching events in the capital with a growing sense of anger and bewilderment. How could Ferranti have been voted into the League if they did not even meet two basic conditions – their name and their ground? For the conspiracy theorists in the north this was yet more proof that the whole process had been a stitch-up from clubs in the south who simply did not want the cost and hassle of playing Highland teams such as Elgin or Inverness Thistle. Either of these two teams, for example, could have slotted into the Second Division with very little need for change or upheaval. It must be conceded that the Highland teams had a point, and one that seemed to be growing in force as the new season approached. This barely-disguised disgust at the entire election process simply heightened Meadowbank's sense of isolation. At least, though, the officials and players had one positive thing to look forward to – the start of the football season itself. Surely that at least could not be as bad as this summer of hell. Could it?

Despite the lurching crises of the summer, there were some favourable outcomes from the League's conditions on entry to the Second Division. The most important of these was the new ground at Meadowbank Stadium. City Park had been a happy ground for the old Ferranti team, and it had been handily placed for the main company at Crewe Toll where many of the players, officials and supporters still worked. It also had good memories as the venue for Thistles' first forays into the Scottish Cup, and a ground that it had shared with Hibs' third team – giving some of the Thistle young players a tantalising glimpse of a possible footballing future at a higher level.

Yet despite these attractions, it was a rundown and sparsely-equipped ground and had only been acceptable to the SFA after Tom Hart's generous gesture in fencing in one side of the windswept grounds. Though decades before Edinburgh City had played league football there, City Park would now need a major overhaul to enable Second Division football to be seen there again.

By contrast, Thistle's move to the Meadowbank Stadium gave them more than just their new name – but the best-equipped sports arena in the Second Division.

The stadium had been built for the recent Commonwealth Games, which had been formally opened by the Duke of Kent on 2 May 1970. It had been built on the site of Old Meadowbank once the home of Edinburgh speedway team the Monarchs and also, more sadly, the one-time home of Leith Athletic FC. Leith had moved to that ground from Portobello after the Second World War and following a chequered history as a League club. Nor was Old Meadowbank to prove a much happier site for the old club. In 1953 Leith had declared that they were unhappy at the state of their division – the old Division C (north and east) – and said they wanted to leave. They saw no reason why they could not still remain part of the Scottish League, however. The League saw it differently, and in August 1953 Leith were duly expelled. Apart from a few Scottish Cup games over the year or so, that was that for Leith. Meanwhile Meadowbank could only hope that this was not a bad omen for them as they played over the ghosts of the old Leith club. (In 1996 the name Leith Athletic FC reappeared in the form of a new community club that runs an amateur side and many youth teams for youngsters in the Port of Leith and surrounding areas.)

Whatever the history of the site, this new stadium certainly boasted some excellent facilities for a small club such as Meadowbank Thistle. Its seating capacity was well over 20,000, though for football matches only the main stand – which had 7,500 seats – was used. Unusually – if not uniquely – for the Second Division the ground had an electronic information board to display scores and result. The 25-acre complex in all boasted a 400m racetrack, an athletics training area, a 250m cycling Velodrome, three all-weather tennis courts and state-of-the-art floodlights. Indoors there were three large multi-purpose sports halls; two smaller practice halls, squash courts, a combat room, two lounges, a cafeteria, and even a film/lecture theatre. These were the kind of facilities that most Second Division – and many First Division – clubs could only dream about.

Therefore, while some Ferranti stalwarts may have regretted the passing of City Park, few could deny the scale and quality of the many facilities Meadowbank now found at the £2.8million Commonwealth stadium.

In one sense, though, the very scale of the London Road Stadium was to become something of a problem over the years to come. Its origin as an athletics track meant that the football playing area – which had a top quality surface – was very remote from the fans in the main stand. The vastness of the stadium in relation to Thistle's likely fan base was always going to make it hard to create an intense atmosphere in the ground. The fact that fans were so far from the players made this even harder. The standing joke was that should there ever be a pitch invasion by home fans, by the time they reached the playing area they would be too tired to cause any trouble.

Then there were the rooms and seemingly endless corridors behind the playing areas. Manager John Bain later admitted that some of his players lost themselves in the complex during the early days of the club's tenure. It certainly took some months before the players, officials and fans felt that the cavernous stadium felt like home'. Some, to be honest, never did. The ground would always be hard to love, and was known – not entirely affectionately – among Scottish football fans as the 'Concrete Lavvy Pan'. For the original Ferranti fans, of course, the new ground was further away from the main Ferranti stronghold at Crewe Toll and the old City Park at Pilton. Meadowbank not only had a new name and a new ground, but a new catchment area. Within a few short months the entire character of the club had undergone a huge change.

One of the traditional Ferranti qualities had been team spirit and the ability to pull together through hard times. Despite the many changes, the 'gang of four' in charge of the club – Blacklaw, Bain, Cowan and Mill – were determined that this at least should not change. They had, after all, chosen to keep most of the players who had been with Ferranti in the last couple of seasons, including for their high-profile cup-ties with Elgin and Partick Thistle. These included their highly rated goalkeeper Derek Gray, veteran centre back Alan Robertson, winger Jim Sivewright and their star striker Ian Martin. With manager and coach – Bain and Glasson – also the same as before, at least on the playing field there was continuity for the season. Meanwhile Bain and Mill were both allowed by their employer Ferranti to work full time on football matters, and they even made use of an office at the company's Edinburgh HQ from which to run the club.

For the players, training sessions were stepped up in readiness for the expected higher standards they would face. The level of training was still limited, however, by the fact that most of the players were strictly part-timers who had full-time jobs elsewhere an who played still for the pleasure rather than the financial rewards – of which it must be admitted there were very few in the Scottish division at that time. (A Thistle player was lucky if they collected as much as £5 a week for playing for the club; meanwhile manager John Bain was actually prohibited by his employers Ferranti from taking any payment, and so managing the team actually cost him money.)

However, Bain and Glasson enjoyed putting the players to work and as the first games approached, and there was a feeling of anticipation at the new club.

Meadowbank's dismal summer would not quite go away, however. The club had arranged to play a Celtic XI at Meadowbank Stadium on August 5 in a Monday evening fixture, the last warm-up match before the season began. Unfortunately, for Meadowbank, however, they had chosen the same night that Hibernian were scheduled to play a home match against Nijmegen. Leith police immediately put a stop to Meadowbank's plans. It might only have been a Celtic XI, but the Glasgow team always attracted a great deal of interest wherever they played in Scotland, and senior police officers felt they could not cope with policing the two games in two nearby stadiums, Meadowbank and Easter Road, on the same evening. Apparently they were worried about the effect on traffic caused by crowds at Meadowbank Stadium, a concern that did not usually loom large for Leith police. Thistle were forced to cancel the game, and instead arrange a practice match against other opposition behind closed doors, hardly ideal preparation for their first season in league football. Manager Bain tried to put a brave face on the setback, but even he could not hide the feeling at Meadowbank that the gods were against them. 'Nothing seems to be going right for us,' he conceded to reporters, 'but we'll plug on because there is genuine enthusiasm among the players, who have kept fit through the summer.'

A few days later, and Meadowbank had a chance to test that enthusiasm and that fitness. The club's first competitive match as a league team was in the League Cup, and it was a tie against Albion Rovers on 9 August 1974. The match was played at Meadowbank Stadium and it was a Friday evening. Thistle had successfully lobbied to have the match switched because Hibs were playing at home on the Saturday, and the club rightly felt that the competition for a crowd might be a little one-sided.

As it was, Meadowbank officials were delighted to see an excellent crowd arriving at the ground on the evening of the match. The fans were charged 30 pence a head, with pensioners required to hand over just 20 pence. There were other incentives too. A blonde 'go go' dancer – they were all the rage at the time- known as 'Wanda' entertained the crowd before the match, and local disc jockey and Ferranti employee Norman Mathieson played the hit sounds of the Seventies. ('Wanda' became something of a legend in that first season – the first question opposition officials and fans asked when Thistle travelled away was 'Did you bring the Go-Go- girl with you?') More prosaically, the club gave out programmes free of charge for this historic occasion. The only ingredient missing from the evening was the result. Thistle put out their strongest team for the tie, a line up that went: Derek Gray in goal, Dave Cathcart, Alan McDonald, Ken Bell, Alan Roberston, Neil Nisbet, Robert Scobie, Derek Fotheringham, Ian Martin, George Hall, and Jim Sivewright. The substitutes were Charlie Crawford and Dennis McGurk. The Thistle side took a while to settle into the game, though as it wore on they began to feel more relaxed and string a few passes together. Sivewright and Martin impressed those onlookers who had not seen this side before, as did goalie Gray – at least until the 58th minutes. That was when he made his only mistake of the game by misjudging a cross, leaving it clear for Rovers striker Dickson to head into the Thistle net.

However, a 1-0 defeat in their first match as a league club was certainly no disgrace, and nor was the performance. The manager John Bain conceded his players had been nervous and had perhaps lacked the 'professionalism and guile' needed to win, but declared himself happy enough with the display. With pleasing candour he added: 'At this stage it is all largely experimental.'

Rovers, too, seemed content with their night's work. The gate had raised £1,200 and the visitors were more than happy with their cut. Indeed, it prompted chairman Tom Fagan (a champion of Ferranti's cause) to take a sideswipe at those critics who believed a Highland Club should have been elected to the League and not the works team. 'We have received one of our biggest cheques in years, proof surely that the League's choice of Meadowbank Thistle and not Inverness Thistle was fully justified.' As ever in football, money talked. Mr Fagan could also have added that his side did not also now face a long and expensive journey home from Inverness; his lobbying on behalf of Ferranti to get the league vote had not been in vain.

As for the fans, they had enjoyed themselves and seen a good night's entertainment. The match had attracted a crowd of 4,000, a large figure by Second Division standards, and greater than Thistle had dared hope. Attendance figure such as this would guarantee Thistle's long-term future in Edinburgh, and the turn out seemed enough to justify confidence in the future. Needless to say, the 4,000 crowd was a record for a football match at the Meadowbank Stadium up to that point. No one could have guessed then that it would remain so until this day.

If even Royal families are allowed an 'annis horribilis' ('terrible year') then it is no great surprise that football clubs can have them as well. It was certainly a description that applied to Meadowbank Thistle's wretched start to the 1974/75 season. Thistle had not been burdened with great expectation from the football world at the start of the season, with just about every neutral (and most at the club itself) expecting a tough start to League football. John Bain and the rest of the management team set the very modest pre-season target of gaining between 12 and 15 points, figures that would practically guarantee a position at the bottom of the table. As it was, Meadowbank threatened to outdo even these bleak forecasts – and in the process became something of a national joke.

The bold facts are that Thistle went for nine games without registering a league point; in other words they lost all nine games. Indeed, when League cup games were added the club lost a total of fourteen matches in a row; and they also conceded 29 goals in the same period. It was by some way the worst record of any league club in Britain. The media quickly made Meadowbank the butt of jokes, while Highland clubs were quick to point out the folly of having allowed such a side to enter the ranks of the League instead of an Elgin or an Inverness. Some of the kinder descriptions of the side during this truly dismal run included 'no-hopers', 'Cinderella men', a 'team miles out of its class' and perhaps most cruel of all 'imposters'. The ultimate insult came from the attention the side's astonishing start to the season attracted outside Scotland. ITV's *World of Sport* programme even devoted a section of their programme to the club's miserable performance. The light-hearted and patronising way in which Meadowbank's form was dealt with was exemplified by a preview of the ITV programme written by journalist Gordon Burnett. He wrote: 'To those of you who think that Jimmy Armfield has problems in taking over Leeds United, I offer a toast this morning: John Bain.

'While Jimmy sorts out his multi-million-pound squad of superstars, John is perming 11 from 17. While Jimmy wonders if Allan Clarke, Joe Jordan or Peter Lorimer will score even more goals for been more points this afternoon, John will be wondering where his next goal – and first point – are coming from.'

Burnett continued that while Leeds were coming into full bloom again, 'John is left holding a Thistle in a bed of nettles. Meadowbank Thistle to be precise. From somewhere near Edinburgh, I understand.' And so the piece went on.

It was crushing stuff for men like Bill Mill, Hugh Cowan, John Bain and Lawrie Glasson, loyal football men who had devoted much of their adult lives to Ferranti and now Meadowbank.

Much fun was made at Bain's expense too when he welcomed the end of weekday fixtures early in the season. 'I'm mighty glad the midweek games are over – two defeats a week can be a bit demoralising,' he was quoted as saying. There was hilarity also at the fact that the club's management claimed goalie Derek Gray was one of the best in the division; despite the side having conceded those 29 goals in nine games.

The worst insult of all, however, came on the pitch when Meadowbank reluctantly took part in the Scottish Qualifying Cup. They had been given a bye in the first round, and in the second round they faced Selkirk. Here at least was the chance for a morale-boosting win against a side whom – as Ferranti – John Bain's men had beaten three times the previous season. Or so their hardy fans assumed. Nothing could have prepared them for what happened next – a 4-1 thrashing by the Borders side. It was, as Bain himself later admitted, a 'humiliating' defeat. This hammering by a non-league team was worse even than the side's 8-1 thrashing by Alloa. The new club had reached rock bottom. Laughed at by the media, scorned by rival fans and clubs, Thistle could see no way out of their nightmare. Had Thistle's first season been a boxing match, the referee would have been tempted to stop the contest there and then.

Nor was it only team's playing performances that attracted unkind attention. One of the side's home games had to be postponed because the pitch was unplayable; not because of bad weather but because the Highland Games had just been held at the stadium and the playing area was still a mess of various white lines. This made playing football on it impossible. On another occasion Thistle had to switch a home match to away at Stranraer because the stadium was required for a religious festival. (To add to the embarrassment, the kick-off then had to be delayed after the Meadowbank team coach got stuck in traffic.) Many in the club – and outside as well – already felt that Thistle had been forced to play second fiddle to the athletics at the stadium and suffered from sharing it with a host of other sporting bodies with whom they competed for space, changing rooms, practice time – and even the toilets. These latest episodes made Thistle feel even more like unwanted guests on their own home ground.

And then it happened. On the very October day that ITV held up Meadowbank's results to national ridicule, the unhappy team from Edinburgh won a game. There was nothing flash or exciting either about the score line or their opponents, as they beat Brechin City away by a solitary goal to nil. But it was a win, and for the first time that season the club could breathe a small sigh of relief. In a way it was appropriate that Brechin were the side that Meadowbank beat. In the previous season Brechin had propped up the Second division with just 14 points and Thistle were expected to emulate this unenviable performance. On the way home from the match, the players and officials stopped for a modest celebration to mark the great event.

The tension that had been slowly building up at the club was suddenly relieved. Spurred into action, John Bain realised that if there were to be more wins ahead his squad had to be strengthened, and he had to be brutal. That same weekend six players were realised from the squad and more were soon to follow. Bain even publicly conceded that he had been a little 'sentimental' in keeping the old Ferranti squad more or less intact. No more. By midway through the season only five of the previous season's regulars were still ever-presents in the Meadowbank line up. These were Derek Gray – who had been watched by Liverpool scouts – Alan Roberston, Jim Sivewright, Charlie Crawford and Ian Martin. Derek Fotheringham, who had joined the club at the start of the season from junior side Drylaw United, was another regular in the team. The rest had been blown away by the increased fitness and skill levels required at Second Division level, as well as the mental pressures that went with playing better quality teams week in, week out. Meanwhile, Bain and Mill boldly recruited new players straight from junior football, and these youngsters started to prosper in their first attempt at senior football. They included 19-year-old Les McVey and Roy Jones.

As so often happens to a team that breaks a long losing streak, Meadowbank suddenly found some form and, more importantly, began to pick up some decent results. Hard-fought wins came against Falkirk – who had recently beaten Hearts in the League Cup – and East Fife quickly followed. Then Thistle travelled to Forfar, knowing that a victory there would take them off bottom place in the Second Division for the first time. This might not turn the season into a success – but at least it would help quell the 'imposter' jibe aimed at them. Any place above bottom would be a vindication of their entry into the League, knowing that there was at least one existing League club with a worse record than them. The coaching staff impressed upon the players the importance of the Forfar game, and the team responded with a 3-1 win. No one got too carried away with this result, but it was nonetheless a significant moment in Meadowbank's young history. Moving from the bottom of the table sent out a message to not just the rest of the division, but to Scottish football as a whole.

As John Bain told reporters at the time: 'we had to put up with a great deal of criticism when we won admission to the Scottish league and now we want to justify our inclusion. The transition from the East of Scotland League to Second Division standards has not been easy, but the players are now starting to believe in themselves. Now confidence is high, I can sense it during training and throughout games.'

Then, revealing the sense of irritation many felt at Meadowbank with the way the club had been portrayed, Bain added: 'I am sure the rest of the Scottish football public will soon have to admit they were too hasty in condemning our entry.'

It was a heart-felt plea from the manager, though deep down he knew that only continuing form on the field would silence the critics. Indeed, the gradual improvement in form soon brought them a total of 13 points from the 13 games after the Brechin win – not bad for a side that could not raise a single point for the first nine matches. By half way through the season the club had also reached its –admittedly very modest – target of between 12 and 15 points for the whole of the season.

Suddenly Meadowbank found themselves being contacted by players who were interested in perhaps joining the new boys of the Second Division. Significantly, too, the media lost interest in the 'Meadowbank joke' story as the team became just another modestly-performing lower division side. One – brief – newspaper story summed up the new mood. Headlined 'The joke is over' it began: 'Have you noticed that they do not make jokes about Meadowbank Thistle any more?'

The management team at Meadowbank deserved all the credit that was now beginning to come their way. The initial derision that greeted Thistle turned in some quarters to genuine admiration for the way Bain, Mill, Glasson and others at the club had kept their dignity and their calm, and had quietly begun to produce results. It was a testament to their powers of motivation skills as much as their footballing acumen that they had not allowed the players to crumble under the withering pressure of the media attacks.

Meadowbank also gratefully acknowledged some kind help from other clubs.

As Bain recalls: 'I got a lot of support from guys like Alex Ferguson at that time. He was at East Stirling and I'd phone him for advice on tactics and stuff. Alex Smith, then at Stirling Albion, was the same.' Both men were to remain friends of Bain.

Motherwell manager Willie McLean and Hearts boss John Haggart also both gave freely of their time in helping Bain and his coach Glasson deal with their team's adjustment to League football.

This sort of selfless generosity from other clubs meant a great deal to Thistle. It highlighted the fact that while the media and the public in general had been quite negative towards the new team, many League clubs had been sympathetic to their plight.

There was even help from one of the legends of British football – the great Bill Shankly. Shankly, who had only recently resigned as manager of Liverpool, had publicly stated that he would be willing to help any club that was struggling in his native Scotland. Eager for all the help they could get, Thistle wrote to Shankly asking for any advice on how to survive in league football. Somewhat to the club's surprise Shankly did not write back – but instead telephoned John Bain and had what was described as a 'long chat'. Perhaps at last the football gods were starting to smile on Meadowbank Thistle.

In January, Thistle suffered another poor run, losing a number of games in a row. But by now the club and players had enough confidence in themselves to pull relatively unscathed. There was no longer the pressure of being characterised as the worst team in British football, and by the end of the 1974/75 season Thistle were starting to pick up more and more points again. They eventually finished with 23 points from 38 League games and were 18th out of the total of 20 teams in the Second Division. Though this was a lowly position, it was two places better than most commentators had predicted and it made clear that at least two teams had worse seasons than Thistle. This was also an unusually competitive season by Second Division standards. The impending reorganisation of the league into three divisions of ten, fourteen and fourteen teams meant there was a tough battle to get into the top six of the Second Division – which would guarantee entry into the new First Division. Thistle were confident that from next season, when the division would contain fourteen more evenly-matched teams, they could hold their own.

Remarkably, Thistle registered a respectable nine wins during their first season, but lost 24 matches. Their biggest problem was an inability to grind out draws in close encounters; they managed only five draws all season. This was doubtless due in part to the inexperience of the squad. Their goal difference did not make happy reading either, as they conceded 87 league goals while scoring a mere 26. Twice they conceded eight goals, once against Alloa and again against Hamilton Academicals. This made it all the more curious that their star player of the season was undoubtedly goalkeeper Derek Gray, who despite all those goals conceded was still attracting interest from bigger clubs. Another success story of the season was a new import, Jimmy Hancock, whom Bain had made captain of the team. The midfielder had previously played with Stirling Albion and also had experience of professional football in England. It was partly due to his experience and energy that Thistle scrambled as many points as they did. A Ferranti 'veteran' who also made it through the season was Ian Martin, though he had found goals much harder to come by in the Second Division than in the East of Scotland League. In fact, the lead marksman for the side in league matches had been Derek Fotheringham, who had originally been signed as a centre half, but had been pressed into action as an emergency centre forward later in the season.

If the performance on the field were modestly promising, then events off it showed even more promise. The crowds inevitably dropped off from the highpoint of their inaugural match at the start of the season. But they still sometimes managed to attract more than a thousand to a home match, and averaged between 600 and 700 a game. This was a considerable improvement on the 300 to 400 Thistle claimed they had been expecting, and was in part due to the fact that they charged only terrace prices for seats in the all-seated main stand. These modest figures may not sound much by modern standards, but for Thistle they were enough. Under the astute financial eye of chairman John Blacklaw, these crowds and other income – mostly from the Founder's Club and fans' payroll payments – were enough to make an impressive profit of £3,500. The club's remarkable financial achievement also included paying off the £1,000 Ferranti loan by end of that same season. Thistle had been in league football for just a year but already had money in the bank and no debts. The club was also feeling happier about its new home at Meadowbank Stadium. Players, officials and fans alike had become used to the vastness of the stadium, and the players in particular were beginning to appreciate some of the excellent facilities on offer. The early-season problems in which football had been forced to take place second best to athletics had been ironed out, in part because of the reduction in midweek games when the two sports clashed. The fact that there would be fewer clubs to play in the following season would also mean more home matches could take place on Saturday afternoons – when there were fewer clashes. Though the temporary lease ran out at the end of the 1974/75 season, both the club and owners Edinburgh Corporation were happy for it to be renewed. Thistle knew that any prospect of returning to their more intimate ground at City Park was ruled out because of the cost of the repair work required.

The clearout of players continued over the summer break, and soon Derek Gray would be the only Ferranti face left in the team. But this high attrition rate was seen as a natural reaction to the physical and footballing demands of League football. All things considered, Meadowbank Thistle had every reason to survey the start of the 1975/76 season with cautious optimism. The team had shown – eventually – that it could hold its own on the field in the Second division, and the reduction in size for next season's division would surely make life slightly easier. Meanwhile the club boasted ground facilities and a bank balance that would be the envy of many other Second Division clubs.

The air of calm assurance was short-lived, however. Having been manager of Ferranti and then Meadowbank Thistle for 23 years, John Bain dramatically resigned on the eve of the new season. It seemed that a behind-the-scenes power struggle at the club had abruptly become public.

4

Learning the Ropes

THE ABRUPT DEPARTURE OF JOHN Bain as manager took everyone connected with the club by surprise. For just about as long as anyone could remember, Bain had been in charge of the club's senior team; since 1953 to be precise.

Now, after twenty unchallenged years as boss, Bain had quit on the eve of Meadowbank's second season in league football. No one outside the club could have had any idea that Bain was preparing to leave the club he had served for so long.

The headline writers in the Scottish press certainly got it right when they declared 'Bain shocker' and 'Bain in quit shock' After all, he had been one of the driving forces – along with Bill Mill and Hugh Cowan – to push the team into the Second division when the chance arose. He had seen the team through the trauma of an appalling early run of form, and then taken the team to the respectable heights of 23 points and 18th position in their first league season. With so much hard work accomplished, why would he choose to quit now? It was a reasonable question and one posed by fans and sports writers alike.

The official verdict given on Bain's resignation by club chairman John Blacklaw was that it was for 'personal reasons' but this was no more than the usual diplomatic varnish that club chairmen applied to such situations. The truth was, as some newspapers reported, that Bain was unhappy with 'interference' in his management of the team by a member of the club's committee, and this had caused him to quit. As he told a newspaper: 'Obviously a lot of back-stabbing and sniping goes on and someone has to take the pats on the back or the boot on the backside is things go wrong.

'But this man was interfering with my job as manager and the committee refused to take any action. I took this as a vote of no confidence and felt I had no alternative but to resign.'

These measured but tough words revealed something of the anger that Bain felt at the way he had been treated by sections of the club, a club whose very existence he had helped to shape over the last twenty years. It was no surprise, therefore, that the former manager refused John Blacklaw's offer of a place on the committee. 'This would have been more or less the same situation, I just couldn't join them on a point of principle.'

Though Bain was careful not to name the committee member with whom he had fallen out, that person was club secretary Bill Mill and another of the so-called gang-of-four who had led Thistle into league football. Mill and Bain had known each other for many years. Both were long time employees of Ferranti and both men had both played and helped to run the football team since the time they joined the East of Scotland League in the 1950s. The two men had always got on well, and were to do so again in later years. At that time, however, the stress involved in changing the club's name, switching grounds and especially that disastrous start to their first season had taken its toll on relations between the pair. Some of the strain was caused by Bain's initial decision at the start of the 1974/75 decision to keep faith with the Ferranti players who had brought them this far. Though this did not work out, Bain has always argued that it was fair to give these players the chance to make it in league football.

The main argument, though, was simply over whether one man – the manager – should be allowed to run the selection and tactics as he saw fit. For someone like Bill Mill, who had been so intimately connected with the club for so many years, it was hard to resist making suggestions, observations, and trying to influence selection. As far as Bain was concerned, however, only one person could and should accept responsibility (and blame) for running the team and that was the manager. During the build up to the 1975/76 season Bain had consulted men whose opinions he valued and trusted. These included Sir John Toothill, the Honorary President of the club and former general manager of Ferranti in Scotland, who advised Bain not to throw away all his hard work, and to stay as manager. Another was Bain's friend Alex Ferguson – a man who has since shown he knows a thing or two about football management – and who also tried to dissuade the Meadowbank manager from quitting. Bain was almost convinced, but in the end decided the committee had lost confidence in him and felt he had to go.

Bain admitted he would be sad to leave the players with whom he had forged a close link in adversity. 'We had a good harmony going and things were just picking up,' he said.

However, there were other reasons too why Bain felt that quitting his position was the right thing to do. His position as manager was of course unpaid and was therefore necessarily, as he later admitted, something of a 'hobby'. His employers Ferranti had been extremely tolerant in giving him time to concentrate on the football side, to the extent where he was almost a full-time manager. But inevitably his work as a production engineer at the company had suffered – a clash of interest that would continue with other personnel at the club after Bain's departure. Now aged 50, Bain knew he had to concentrate on his career for his and his family's sake. All this made his decision to end his 20-year reign as Thistle's manager slightly easier to bear. Nor did Bain sever his connections with the club; he continued to watch matches from the touchline – this time as a fan – and later took up Sir John's wise suggestion that he joined the board of directors of the club. The John Bain era at Thistle, however, had finally come to an end.

The club had little time to dwell on the departure of its veteran manager. On the very day that Bain had quit, the club announced that it had signed three new players for the coming season, Alan Duthie, who had been released by Celtic, and junior club players Robert Kilgour and Billy Harper. The strengthening of the club had to continue if Meadowbank were to improve on the previous season's modest achievements, now that they were in the new Second Division (effectively the Third Division) with fourteen teams. The team would once more be built around the goalkeeper Derek Gray, the real star of the side, and skipper Jimmy Hancock whose midfield toil and leadership had helped achieve respectability the previous season. The problem, as ever, would be who would score the goals. Ian Martin, who had been Ferranti's top marksman for three season in the East of Scotland League, had suffered from injuries and had yet to come to terms with the greater demands of Second Division football.

As for the day-to-day running of the team, there was still some continuity despite Bain's departure. The main coaching duties remained with Ferranti veteran Lawrie Glasson, though he was now aided by another Ferranti employee Jeff Skeldon. However, for the time being Meadowbank appointed no new manager to replace Bain. Chairman Blacklaw said they would be making an appointment but were in no hurry to do so. In the meantime, the recruitment of players and team selection was taken on by the club's committee. This committee included Will Mill, the club secretary and vice-chairman and former player Hugh Cowan, while a third was yet another Ferranti employee Alec Ness.

Committees have their place in football, as they do in all sports and other areas of life. But when it comes to the day-to-day running of a side, they are far from ideal. Players and fans alike need to know who is in charge. The compromise decisions that committees tend to make can seem confusing and lacking in clarity when it comes to the direction of a football team. It is hard to image, for example, Sir Alex Ferguson picking his Manchester United team at the behest of a committee.

So it was perhaps no great surprise that Meadowbank endured another miserable start to a season. Though there was thankfully no repeat of the previous year's nine game losing streak, the first twenty league games yielded the Edinburgh side a mere eleven points, including just four wins. Once again, the new boys of Scottish football were rooted to the bottom of the Second Division. This time, however, they did not have the 'excuse' of being debutants in the league, not did they attract the same sympathy as before. Perhaps inevitably, some of the old mutterings about Thistle and their worthiness to play league football began to return again. They had now played 71 games in all competitions since becoming Meadowbank Thistle and had won just 15 of them.

One of the continuing causes of complaints against Meadowbank was their stadium. Though the arena had a great playing surface and some fine athletics facilities, it had not been designed with football in mind. Visiting clubs complained that the dressing rooms were crowded for a full team with substitutes and there was no room for even a pre-match rub-down. The 'big squeeze' was some how critics described the Meadowbank experience. There were complaints too that the facilities to deal with injured players were poor, and that some players had to receive attention for their wounds while lying on the floor. Another gripe was about the toilets – which footballers resented having to share with people playing other sports such as badminton in the arena. East Stirling manager Dan McLindon summed up some of the widely held views about the ground. 'Meadowbank has a great playing surface but the dressing rooms are foreign to football. We had to put the team hampers in the showers and use them as a table!'

Chairman John Blacklaw rejected the complaints about the facilities, but nonetheless they persisted. And when these drawbacks were added to the admitted remoteness of the pitch from the fans, it was not hard to see why Meadowbank Stadium was a less than popular venue for many clubs.

There was also continued unhappiness from Highland clubs that Ferranti/Meadowbank had been chosen ahead of one of their number, especially given the continuing struggle of the Edinburgh side to make the grade so far. John MacDonald, chairman of Inverness Thistle – who lost out on the league vote to Ferranti – was asked for his verdict on Meadowbank as they lay at the bottom of the table at the end of 1975. 'Good luck to them,' was his gracious comment. He added: 'They got in, we didn't – but I still think the clubs who voted for Meadowbank took the easy way out.'

On a more personal note, the halfway point of the 1975/76 season also saw a sad end to the Meadowbank career of Ian Martin. Martin, who was still only 26, had been the golden boy of the Ferranti team and had scored 35 goals in their last season before joining the Football League. Yet in the 1974/1975 year in the Second Division he had managed just five. The player himself was wise enough to admit that the step up in standard had been considerable. 'That's what can happen when you face fitter and faster players,' he commented sadly. Then in the new season injury had kept him out of the side and early in 1976 he was granted a free transfer at his own request. It was a disappointing way for Martin's senior career with Thistle to end, and somehow symptomatic of the way in which the club was still struggling to come to terms with the demands of league football. As a sports editorial in the Sunday Mail commented at the time: 'Meadowbank Thistle are hardly entitled, in all honesty, to look back on their brief career in the Scottish league with any special satisfaction.'

True, the same editorial then stated that the club had nothing 'to be ashamed of…or to apologise for' and that there was 'much affection' for them – in Edinburgh, at least.

Yet, it was impossible to escape the feeling that Meadowbank's birth pains as a league club were lasting a long time.

It was around this point – early in 1976 – that the club's committee decided to appoint someone to the manager's slot that had been vacant since John Bain's abrupt pre-season departure. The committee had tried its best to direct the shape and make-up of the team, but inevitably the lack of one person in charge had been in handicap.

The man chosen to take on the job at this difficult time was Alec Ness.

Ness was already on the committee overseeing the team, so he was not a new face, and knew the strengths and weaknesses of the players from first hand experience. The Ferranti senior engineer also had a significant track record in football. He had been a scout for Falkirk and East Fife and knew football and players at all levels in Edinburgh inside out. Ness had also been chairman of the club's supporters clubs and so was a familiar figure to the fans. Though he had no direct managerial experience at anything like this level, Ness was at least guaranteed the full support of his fellow committee members. This would ensure there would be no repeat of the behind-the-scenes row's that had led to the previous manager's departure. With Glasson and Skeldon in charge of the coaching, there was still a strong feeling of continuity about the management team.

Ness' immediate aim was to continue the all-out youth policy at Meadowbank, a clear sign that they were aiming for future success rather than an instant fix to their current mediocre form. Already the committee had drastically changed the age profile of the team in the first few months of the season. The average age was slashed from 30 under the Bain regime to just 20. In one recent game only two of the players had been aged 21 or over – an astonishing statistic. Ness was now promising that this youth policy – which he had helped develop with his committee members – would continue. 'We are satisfied with the progress which has bee made in this direction and will maintain this policy,' he added on the day he took over as the new manager. The club hoped that Ness would be around for some years to make sure this emphasis on young players came good.

The mood of optimism that youth was the answer could not however disguise the disappointment when Thistle ended their second season in the Second Division rooted at the bottom.

While Alec Ness was finding his feet as manager, the club had other matters to handle. One was the curious story of the banned ball-boys. When Thistle had first moved to the Meadowbank Stadium and joined league football, one of their first acts had been to instigate a regular rota of ball boys at the ground. Indeed, at the very first game that Thistle played on the ground in August 1974, one of the ball boys had been a ten-year-old John Robertson, the future star of Hearts and Newcastle – and more recently on the coaching staff at Livingston. (His abiding memory is being given a can of soft drink – Tizer – and 10 pence for a bus fair which he spent on a hamburger supper on the way home.)

Ballboys were not a luxury or a public relations exercise at Meadowbank Stadium – they were a necessity. The vastness of the stadium meant that valuable minutes could be wasted during a game while someone fetched the ball; in that sense it was a little like parks football. Therefore, the ballboys helped preserve the momentum of a match. Unfortunately, this practical benefit of ballboys made little difference when it came to the law. For it was pointed out that under a local by-law in Edinburgh, children under 16 could not be employed within the city – and being given a soft drink and a bus fare in turn for fetching a ball was deemed employment. The by-law had been passed in line with the Protection of Children Scotland Act 1937 and had clearly had the laudable aim of stopping the exploitation of children. Unfortunately, it stopped them from being ballboys at Meadowbank Stadium as well. The Lothian and Borders police insisted they were sympathetic to Meadowbank's need for help, but said that they would be obliged to bring charges if the club continue to use ballboys. The club was therefore forced to stop using those under 16 – and in reality it has never been easy to find youngsters aged 16 or more to work as ballboys. In 1976, local councillors tried to help Meadowbank by getting the law changed by making allowance for the case of ballboys. In the meantime, though, John Blacklaw warned that the club would suffer as a result of the ban. He said: 'since the ban has been applied, I have had to tell referees some of the difficulties we have encountered. Visiting teams, too, without first-hand knowledge of the problems, have often thought that play was being interrupted too often when the ball is out of play.'

Alec Ness's reign as manager was to last just a year before he resigned in early 1977. The reason he gave was a familiar one to those on the club's committee – pressure of work. Ness was a senior engineer with Ferranti and inevitably found that his position as manager conflicted with his obligations to the company. Both jobs took up too much time and one, ultimately, had to go.

Ness had done a respectable if unspectacular job as manager and had at least gone out on a relative high note. By January 1977 they had earned 22 points in the Second Division. This was more than they had ended up with in the 1975/76 season and only one fewer than they had reached in their first league season – in a division with six more teams. He could also therefore take credit for the side ending 11th out of 14 at the end of the season, their best performance in three attempts. In addition, and as promised, Ness had brought on some promising youngsters at the club, while holding onto stalwarts such as Derek Gray and Jimmy Hancock.

As Ness noted at the time: 'I am sorry to be leaving the club but I feel I have left them with a solid base on which to build. There is a lot of talent there.'

Nonetheless, the club was still languishing towards the lower reaches of the division and it was still proving hard to make a significant breakthrough. This was by no means Ness's fault – the club had few resources to splash out on new signings. Yet there was still a feeling that the club, the third team of Edinburgh, was underachieving.

After Ness's departure, it was proving hard to find – or at least to keep – a manager at the club. Thistle had an understandable desire to keep the manager an in-house appointment. They still saw themselves as a family club who attracted lots of families to watch them, and the biggest family of all were the Ferranti staff. Unfortunately, anyone the club chose to be manager and who already worked for Ferranti would be in the same position as John Bain and Alec Ness – trying to serve two demanding masters at the same time. The other option of course was to look outside the club and the confines of Ferranti, though if they got the choice wrong it risked upsetting the more intimate atmosphere of the club.

These dilemmas perhaps explain why, for the second time in its brief history, Meadowbank now chose to play on without a manager. Once again the committee ran the show, with vice-chairman Hugh Cowan to the fore, while the ever-present coach Lawrie Glasson was in charge of day-to-day playing matters. This unorthodox arrangement saw out the rest of the 1976/77 season and into the start of 1977/78.

The new season started brightly enough for the manager-less club, as Thistle soon registered an early season 2-1 win at East Stirling. The following month, September, saw two welcome milestones too as Thistle beat Brechin City 5-3. This was the club's biggest score since joining the league; meanwhile one of the goals, from Tom Downie, was the club's 100th in its new existence as Meadowbank Thistle. Even in this free-scoring game, however, there had been warning signs. Having gone 4-0 down, Brechin pulled three back to make for a tight finish until a late penalty from the ever-reliable Jimmy Hancock made the game safe. And indeed, the positive start to the league campaign merely flattered to deceive. There were a few familiar names around the team still, Derek Gray, the afore-mentioned Jimmy Hancock, Steve Hancock and Derek Fotheringham. But even the experienced hands could not stop Thistle now enduring one of those now horribly familiar periods in the league campaign. By Christmas, the side had won just three games out of twenty, and were lucky to be as high as second from bottom in the Second Division.

The Meadowbank committee was now aware that the team could no longer be allowed to drift in this way, and that they would need to appoint a new, dedicated manager. Moreover, John Blacklaw, Bill Mill, and Hugh Cowan were now resigned to choosing someone from outside the Ferranti 'family'. Their choice was Willie Macfarlane.

Willie MacFarlane seemed a shrewd appointment for a club in Meadowbank's position. A former player for Hibs and Raith Rovers, and after spells in charge at Hawick Royal Albert and Stirling Albion, he had been manager at the Easter Road club for 15 months, before moving full time into the building business. Now, seven years later, MacFarlane was keen to get back into football and Thistle offered him a great chance. The former Hibs man knew Edinburgh football inside out and was a popular figure in footballing circles. MacFarlane also had experience in the transfer market, having sold Peter Marinello and Peter Cormack while at Hibs for a total of £200,000, and having spent £100,000 on signing players, though this money-wheeling experience was unlikely to be required immediately at Meadowbank.

It was in any case a golden opportunity to get back into league football and Macfarlane seized it with both hands. He told *Ferranti News*, who still kept a close eye on Meadowbank's fortunes: 'Football was my life and I couldn't resist coming back.'

The size of Macfarlane's task was soon apparent as in his very first game in charge Meadowbank lost by four goals at Cowdenbeath. However, the new boss refused to be disheartened and soon began to make use of the talents at his disposal.

One of these was a youngster called Jackie Smyth. The 5ft 5 in Belfast-born striker had arrived at Hearts the previous June for a month's trial, but was released. Though the 18-year-old was snapped up by Meadowbank, he had spent most of his time languishing on the bench until MacFarlane arrived. Aware of the teenager's natural talent, the new boss gave Smyth a run in the side, and he was rewarded with some impressive goal scoring – notably in the Scottish Cup.

After Thistle's initial run-in with the SFA in their first season – when they had to play in the Qualifying Cup and lost to Selkirk – Thistle had made little impact in the competition. This year however Thistle were to make more of an impression. A bye in the first round led to a second round clash with Stirling Albion, whom they saw off 2-1 – with Smyth getting his name on the scoresheet.

The third round brought a much-anticipated home match against Inverness Caley, a free-scoring Highland club. Appalling weather and a muddy pitch did not dampen the excitement for a match and the Stadium attracted a good crowd of 3,000. The players did not disappoint and MacFarlane was particular delighted when Smyth scored twice – both of them brilliantly taken – to beat Caley 2-1. The goals brought Smyth's tally to four in three games and more importantly ensured that Meadowbank had got through to the final 16 of the cup for the first time. The manager told reporters after the game that Smyth had helped to turn around their season. 'Jackie has had a hand in every goal we've scored in recent weeks.'

He also singled out the 'skilful' play of versatile winger/fullback Tom

O'Rourke, Tom Downie and Kenny Davidson. (O'Rourke was soon to become the first Meadowbank player to leave in a cash deal when Motherwell paid £15,000 for him.)

MacFarlane was also exultant about his own return to football. 'It's great to be back and to have this bit of success so early.'

The game highlighted the ever-changing fortunes of football at whichever level it is played. Alex Main's Caley team had been full of optimism for the trip to Edinburgh, and some observers felt they were unlucky not to get a draw. As it was, a bad day got even worse when blizzards disrupted the side's train journey back up north. The train eventually limped into Inverness at 4.30am, after a ten-hour journey.

Meanwhile Meadowbank were delighted that, though they was still struggling in the league, the team was able to perform well in the cup as it had done before in the old days of Ferranti. If nothing else the cup run would guarantee some extra money for the team coffers, and there was no expensive return match against Inverness Caley to undertake. Yet though MacFarlane prepared his team thoroughly for the fourth round match, against Morton, they were outclassed by the Greenock side and lost comfortably. This left Meadowbank with just the league to concentrate on, but their frustratingly inconsistent Second Division form persisted to the end of the season. One of the problems was the team's alarming ability to leak goals on a regular basis. Though Derek Gray was usually outstanding in goal the defence and midfield ahead of him was far less effective. Thistle managed a clean goal sheet only a handful of times all the season. One of these was a 0-0 draw against highly-rated Raith Rovers in which MacFarlane had played Steve and Jimmy Hancock alongside Tom Downie in midfield to shore up the centre of the team. Jimmy Hancock, in contrast to the team's overall performance, was the very model of consistency and fitness, and had proved himself to be the ideal club player. In three seasons out of four Hancock made more appearances in a Thistle shirt than anyone else, and for two years he was joint top scorer (admittedly the totals were just eight in 1976/77 and six in 1977/78, a measure of the team's problems in scoring goals consistently). When Hancock was absent from the last two games of Thistle's 1977/78 season they were the first only games he missed through injury in three years. These last two games, in fact, underlined the problems that MacFarlane faced as a manager. The first of the matches had seen the team come away with a fine win at Falkirk, who had been fighting hard for promotion. Yet the next game, at home, the same Thistle performed miserably to lose 3-2 to Cowdenbeath.

It was a familiar pattern. Every now and again Meadowbank would pull off an outstanding result, but for much of the rest of the time they struggled to make an impact.

In an effort to change his side's fortunes, MacFarlane kept trying to unearth new talent and signed a number of youngsters he hoped would make the grade. These included 17-year-old David Ballantine, from Craigmount, and 16-year-old schoolboy Gordon Fraser, who had unfortunately been burdened with the tag 'Puskas' by an over-eager schoolteacher. A third player, and another from the successful Tartan junior team in Edinburgh, was 16-year-old midfielder David Conroy.

Yet despite the bold moves to recruit young talent, the 1978/79 season had a familiar feel to it. For the fourth season in a row, Thistle struggled to make any real impression in the Second Division.

Once again, however, they did make an impression in the Scottish Cup. In the first round they had been drawn – again – against Inverness Caley at Meadowbank Stadium. The Highland side were out for revenge after the previous year's result, and nearly achieving it by pushing Meadowbank all the way to a 1-1 draw. The hard-fought game was not without its lighter moments either. The stadium's electronic scoreboard somehow managed to welcome the teams and fans to 'Calais' rather than Edinburgh. Meanwhile, the same scoreboard evidently got confused about which Inverness side was playing and flashed up the names of Inverness Thistle players – instead of those from neighbours Caley.

The match also highlighted just how expensive football can be. The crowd of just 662 paid little more than £240 for the game, leaving each club with a little over £100 each after deductions. Yet Caley's two-day stay in the capital and travel expenses cost the Highland club around £900. Even allowing for a travel subsidy from the SFA, the drawn match cost Caley around £700; while Meadowbank could expect a similar shortfall for the return game. At least they won the replay, setting up a 2-1 win against Stenhousemuir in the second round and a similar result against Spartans in the third.

It was now that Meadowbank experienced the financial flipside of the Cup; they had now secured a lucrative fourth round tie against fellow Edinburgh side Hibernian. Thistle had been drawn at home, but the match was switched after consultation between the clubs to Easter Road. The result therefore might have been predictable – a 6-0 drubbing by Hibs – but the crowd was a healthy 6,000. This of course guaranteed a decent profit on the day for Thistle, who did not even have any significant travel expenses to find. It was a welcome boost to a team that was run on a shoestring, even though under John Blacklaw's chairmanship the club had an enviable reputation for financial prudence. The problem was that without a more successful team, the club would find it hard to raise additional revenue. Home crowds of under 1,000 for league matches was unlikely to swell club's coffers (in fact the average home attendances for the seasons from 1974/75 to 1979/80 were 677, 463, 574, 503 and 464 which suggested that far from growing, the fan base was slowly diminishing). Yet without more money now, how could the club hope to attract the kind of players it needed to improve results and improve its profile? It was the kind of Catch-22 that was to dog Meadowbank for many years. For the second time in its existence, the club finished bottom of the Second Division at the end of the 1978/79 season. It seemed that results were getting worse, not better.

The season saw the end of an era on the playing side with the abrupt retirement of goalkeeper Derek Gray. Gray had been one of the stars of the new league era at Thistle, and one of the very few who had successfully made the transition from the East of Scotland league to Second Division. Gray had continued to play football at this level for fun, but his day job – he was a tax inspector – was taking up more and more time. Now aged 30, and recently married, he knew it was time to hang up his gloves and concentrate on his career instead.

His departure left a void at the club, a gap that was immediately filled by Bonnyrigg Rose goalie Charlie Sinclair and later by Derek Neilson. Gray's absence also brought home the rapid turnover of players that Macfarlane had overseen. By January 1980, in fact, only three players remained from when the former Hibs boss had taken over. The new star of the team was now top goal scorer John Jobson (whose brother Richard was lead singer with Scottish band The Skids). Jobson became the club's first double figure marksman when he scored 17 goals in the 1979/80 season. This rapid influx of talent coincided with an upturn in fortunes in the Second Division. Already, by that same period January 1980, Thistle had picked up 22 points from 22 games, a far better rate of return than in previous seasons. The principle reason for this was a major improvement in form at Meadowbank Stadium. Though the vast arena was still far from being an impregnable fortress, the club had only lost one of its first eleven games there.

One intriguing away fixture that season had again underlined the extent to which Second Division sides were perennially concerned about travel costs – a concern shared just as much by Thistle as anyone else. The game was at Montrose on New Year's Day, 1980. The referee Jim Renton had wisely gone to the ground early and quickly realised that the pitch was so frozen there was no chance of the game-taking place. Unfortunately, in the days before mobile phones and pagers, there was no way to alert the away team – Thistle – until their team bus turned up at Links Park. The coach came at 1.30pm and Renton went to inform manager Willie MacFarlane of the news about the frozen pitch. MacFarlane, however, had already made up his mind. Walking across the rock-hard pitch he informed the referee that he could not postpone the game. The reason was simple; the club could not afford another coach trip if the fixture was rearranged. MacFarlane was, as Renton recalls, very forceful in his view. So much so that the referee reluctantly agreed to play the match on one condition; that no tackling was allowed on the treacherous surface. An equally reluctant Montrose agreed to the conditions and so one of the more remarkable games in Scottish League history took place. Neither side tackled and the game ended without a single foul – and in an entertaining 3-3- draw. The game delighted the fans, Willie MacFarlane, and the football authorities – it was the only game that survived the weather that day. Yet, whether league and SFA officials would have been so happy had they know about the real circumstances of the fixture is another matter.

The 1979/80 season saw yet another decent cup performance too. This included beating Stranraer 2-1 in a replay at home after managing a draw at Stair Park. Once more, Thistle had now been set up with a lucrative game for the next round – home to Hibs again. The home team this time seriously considered keeping this game at Meadowbank Stadium, but after consulting the city council and police the venue was switched. This time, though, the game was played at Hearts' ground at Tynecastle. The fixture, held in 26 January, attracted more than 8,400 fans – a huge crowd for Thistle and one doubtless boosted by the presence in the Hibs side of a player called George Best. The financial rewards could have been even greater if Thistle had managed to snatch a late equaliser to force a replay, as a subdued Hibs side won by just a single goal. At last, Thistle seemed to be producing solid form in both the league and the cup.

If events on the field were appearing to get better for Meadowbank, 1980 also saw some interesting plans off the field. Chairman John Blacklaw revealed that the club was considering a move to its own ground, by redeveloping the site of the old swimming pool at Portobello. The club had no chance of financing the estimated £1.25million it would need by itself. However, Blacklaw hoped that the council and private backers might be interested in developing a sports complex on the site, of which the football ground would be the key component. In the end the idea came to nothing, as the right financial backing could not be found, and there was in any case significant local opposition from people who felt that the football club would dominate the leisure centre and who were also unhappy at dealing with the problems of football fans in their area. But the contemplation of the move was significant in showing two things. One was the ambition of Meadowbank, and its realisation that to grow as a club it probably needed its own ground and facilities better suited to a football team. Another was that the discussions were proof of the club's own dissatisfaction with the existing stadium – despite their public claims to the contrary. Though the stadium was in many ways well equipped and modern by most Scottish football standards, it was still hard for Meadow-bank to feel 'at home'. They still had to fight each August and September to play home matches on Saturdays at the stadium, against the competing demands of athletics and other events. Such problems in producing a consistent fixture list made it even harder to grow a loyal fan base.

There was also growing dissatisfaction within the management team as well. Though performances were showing signs of improvement, there were differences behind the scenes between manager MacFarlane and another new face at the club, Terry Christie. Christie had been appointed assistant manager at the club in 1978 soon after MacFarlane's arrival, and for a while the two had worked well enough together. Now, though, the relationship had become more tense as their views on players and team strategy began to diverge.

Perhaps surprisingly, it was MacFarlane who was asked to step aside. It was another setback for Thistle, just at the time when they had seemed on the verge of a breakthrough in performances. Christie was meanwhile appointed caretaker manager while the club's committee decided on a permanent replacement.

In just five seasons Meadowbank had gone through three different managers plus two separate spells in which the club committee ran the team. They were in danger of gaining a reputation as a team that was hard to manage, and as a club split by behind-the-scenes politics. It was important that the Edinburgh club chose their next manager wisely, someone who would command respect and stay at the helm for a long period. The question was, who?

Ferranti won all the trophies in the Lothian welfare league before joining the East of Scotland League, back row, second from left, the late Tommy Learmouth, third from right, John Bain, front row, first on left, Bill Mill, seated last the late Derek Read.

A rare glimpse of an early Ferranti Thistle game as captain John Bain (left in stripes, rugby strip) takes part in the toss in a 1955-56 matches away to Eyemouth United. In those days, the referee wore a blazer.

The victorious Ferranti team that won the 1962-63 east of Scotland Qualifying Cup. Back row, L to R: McGonagle, Glasson, Craig, Cowan, Angus, and Melrose. Front row, L to R: Lawrence, Birrell, Brown, Teasdale and McTiernan.

The Ferranti side of the 1960's. a number of players later found success with bigger clubs.
Front left: Graham Pate – Hibs: next to him, Jackie Landels – Leith Athletic.
Bottom right: Bob Leishman – East Fife.

Past and present Ferranti players at a social event, 1970-71 season, back row, Far right, John Bain, his son Ian is on the back row left. Others present include Lawrie Glasson, Bill Mill, Robin Melrose, and George Smart.

Bill Mill secretary, John Bain, manager and the late Tom Neal, Ferranti works manager, debate the club's new venue and name after their elevation to the Scottish league in 1974-75

Ferranti players and officials celebrate their 6-0 aggregate win after two legs against the Civil Service Strollers in the Scottish Qualifying Cup, 1973-74. They did not know it but it was to be the club's last season under the Ferranti name.

Beaten but not unbowed. The scene moments after the final whistle on 26 January 1980 after Hibernian beat Meadowbank Thistle 1-0 in a Scottish Cup third round tie at Tynecastle. Thistle striker John Jobson is shown shaking hands with Hibs' star recruit – a certain George Best.

The Meadowbank squad at the start of the 1980-81 season. By the end of it however, manager Willie McFarlane, back row left, had been replaced as team boss by his assistant Terry Christie, back row right.

Attendances at the cavernous Meadowbank Stadium were always disappointing. As this photograph of Meadowbank Thistle playing at home to Ayr United on 24 march 1984 shows, average gates remained low.

During their first season in the First Division in 1983-84, Meadowbank enjoyed a memorable League Cup win over Partick Thistle. Here Gordon Smith, (number 10) is seen scoring a vital equaliser against the Firhill side.

Silverware at last! The Meadowbank Thistle squad proudly show off the Club's first senior title in League football after winning the Second Division in 1987-88

Though the move to Livingston in 1995 was controversial among Meadowbank fans, the club was well received in West Lothian. Here club officials accept a 'Good Luck' gift from the fledgling Livingston Supporters club. From L to R: club secretary, Jim Renton, Hugh Cowan, Chairman Bill Hunter, former manager John Bain and Thistle stalwart, Walter Hay.

Meadowbank Thistles first manager has a long standing friendship with Manchester United manager, Sir Alex Ferguson. Sir Alex seen here with John in 2000 when Livingston played Manchester United in a friendly at Livingston.

Livingston skipper Stuart Lovell in action against Motherwell on 5 August 2002, wearing the club's new and controversial home strip that for the first time did not feature the side's traditional black and amber; the old colours were restored for the next season.

The famous Livi Lions celebrate the club's first foray into the first round of the UEFA Cup when they played away at Sturm Graz on 24 September 2003

*Start them young;
youthful Livingston fans
are put through their
paces at one of the
many coaching sessions
that the club provides.*

*A historical
moment. The
exchange of club
pennants as
Livingston
prepare for the
UEFA Cup tie
against Sturm
Graz at the
Arnold
Schwarzenegger
Stadium*

*Fans celebrate the great
moment as Livingston
makes their entrance to
European football
against Sturm Graz.*

5

Success At Last

N MANY WAYS, TERRY CHRISTIE was an unlikely choice for a manager. At the time that Christie took over as caretaker of Meadowbank Thistle, in 1980, he was deputy rector of Trinity Academy. Within eighteen months, he would take over as head teacher of Ainslie Park High School in Edinburgh, the youngest head teacher in Lothian Region at the time. The sober demands of running a school or an academy somehow sat oddly with the manic and magnified pressures of football management.

Yet when Christie took over in temporary control of the Meadowbank team the 37-year-old chemistry graduate was already very experienced in the peculiarities of Scottish football. He had signed for Dundee while still a schoolboy, and while during his five years at Dens Park he never made the breakthrough into first team football, he followed this with spells at Raith Rovers, Hawick Royal Albert and Stirling Albion. Meanwhile Christie's football teaching career started in 1970 when he gained a full certificate from the English coaching school at Durham; the future Leeds and Sunderland boss Howard Wilkinson was a fellow pupil. Not that the piece of paper overwhelmed the graduate Christie.

'In truth coaching certificates don't mean that much,' Christie later conceded. 'It's like passing your driving test. The real driving only starts afterwards. In the business of managing football clubs I am largely,self-taught.' There were useful hands-on tutors along the way, however. It was at Hawick that Christie first played under Willie MacFarlane, and when the latter moved to take charge of Stirling Albion, he took the teacher with him. The manager respected Christie's thoughtful approach to the game. Christie later gained some managerial experience himself, first becoming player-manager and then manager at non-league side Newtongrange Star. It came as no great surprise, therefore, that when MacFarlane took over the reins at Meadowbank in 1978 he asked Christie to join him as assistant manager at the struggling Edinburgh club.

At first the pair had worked well together; MacFarlane had the experience and contacts, and Christie the youthful energy and determination – though he also learnt from the veteran manager's style.

Yet by the 1979/80 season the two men were starting to view the team quite differently and started to disagree on team selection and tactics. MacFarlane meanwhile was under fire on two fronts. One was the pressure of his other work. MacFarlane had become a successful businessman in the building trade and admitted that as he was obliged to pay people to do his work, managing Meadowbank was actually costing him money. The other pressure was the continuing poor league form of the club, who had still to finish higher than 11th out of 14 clubs in the Second Division. In December 1980 they were still scraping along the bottom of the division, with little real sign or hope that results would improve. Perhaps the last straw came in the first round of the Scottish Cup, when Meadowbank played hosts to Highland League side Buckie Thistle (Meadowbank and before them Ferranti had developed a habit of meeting Highland sides in the cup.) It should have been a comfortable win for the Edinburgh league team, but instead the teams drew 2-2 before a crowd of just 400. Even Meadowbank's cup form seemed to be deserting them and now they faced a long and potentially expensive trip up north for the replay.

Under these circumstances, it was a near-certainty that something or someone would give way, and ultimately it was MacFarlane.

The club's handbook was deliciously understated a year or so later when it looked back on the departure of MacFarlane. It said: 'Season 1980/81 saw no great improvement in our League position and following some involved discussions it was agreed that the Manager and the club should part....'

The phrase 'involved discussions' was a polite way of referring to the heated exchanges that took place as MacFarlane – with more that some justification – protested that he had hardly had the resources or indeed the luck necessary to turn the club's fortunes around. At the time of the departure, Chairman John Blacklaw had simply made a brief announcement. In it he suggested that 'Meadowbank Thistle and Willie MacFarlane have terminated amicably their three-year agreement'. The headline writers were nearer the mark when they wrote: 'Meadowbank sack Willie MacFarlane.'

Once again, aside from appointing Christie as caretaker boss, the club showed a curious reluctance to go out into the football world and search for a permanent replacement. In remarks that recalled the management by committee of earlier seasons, Blacklaw stated: 'We intend to give the team a run as things stand and to await developments. No doubt there will be applications because one came in a few weeks ago when there was no hint of a vacancy.'

It may not have been intended, but the statement gave the impression of an employer trying to fill a shop floor vacancy rather than a football club looking for a man to lead its team. At least, however, the club had not reverted to management by committee, the policy it had adopted after the resignations of John Bain and Alec Ness.

Meanwhile MacFarlane himself was quietly philosophical about his departure. 'I had no contract with Meadowbank – just a gentleman's agreement. The club has gone forward in so many ways since I've been there but injuries have been tough on us this season.' He added: 'I'll retain my interest in football in some capacity but there are no definite plans at this moment.'

If this was Thistle's first sacking of a manager in their history, it was a curiously low-key and bloodless one, certainly by modern standards.

Christie now had been given his chance to improve Meadowbank's fortunes, but it was no means clear – from chairman Blacklaw's remarks – whether he was favourite to retain the job full-time. The gap between Newtongrange Star and Second Division football was a substantial one, and while the two years working under Willie MacFarlane had taught Christie a good deal, he was very much on trial for the rest of the season. His first task was to take his players up to play Buckie Thistle in the first round cup replay. It was a game that for reasons of morale – as well as money – they could scarcely afford to lose. Yet Christie's management got off to the worse possible start as Buckie – cheered on wildly by 1300 fans at Victoria Park – ran out 3-2 winners against the Second Division side. As the Meadowbank team glumly made their way back south, it would have taken a brave man to foresee a long future for Terry Christie at Meadowbank.

The Christie approach to management was outlined in an interview he gave to the Times Educational Supplement – not a usual place to find a football manager's comments – in 1982. In it the teacher described how football management, unlike running a school, had to be autocratic in nature. A ten-minute talk at half-time, he pointed out, was not the time to embark on a process of democracy. At the same time, a manger had to be demanding and expect the best – in other words be a bit of a 'nag'. Christie also considered some of the similarities between his work as a teacher and his position as a football boss. 'Running a football team is teaching, only in football they call it coaching and tend to tell a youngster what to do without explaining why.'

In a later interview he would add: 'I've always had very clear ideas of how I want my teams to play and it's been a question of retaining what works and discarding what doesn't.

'I don't believe in shouting and bawling. I get excited during a match but in preparing and dealing with players it's very much a matter of doing things quietly.'

These and other public comments by the Meadowbank boss revealed the existence of a rather more authoritative character than perhaps Christie's usually quiet demeanour may have betrayed. He certainly had an air of authority that was rubbed off on his players. Yet at the same time Christie was clear about where his ultimate priorities lay in his life – and they were not in football. He was deputy rector or head teacher first, football manager second, he explained. Football was his hobby; a valuable hobby that allowed him to keep in touch with other areas of 'real' life outside teaching, but still a hobby. This perhaps also explains why in the same interview Christie said: 'I am under no pressure at Meadowbank.' It is the kind of statement that few if any league managers could make truthfully nowadays. But in Christie's case it may been the reason why he could relax, enjoy the experience and encourage the Thistle team to take shape – all because he felt no pressure. In that sense his teaching and football complemented each other well.

The caretaker manager's first priority was to be taken on permanently. The club had talked about making an appointment at the start of the 1981-82 season. But within weeks of taking the hot seat at Meadowbank Stadium Christie had helped his team to a string of good results, picking up 15 precious league points along the way. If this was not advertisement enough for his talents, then Christie made sure the club knew where he stood by formally requesting to be made permanent boss. In the circumstances, and with team spirit higher than it had been for some while, the club agreed. Chairman Blacklaw confirmed Christie's appointment and promoted veteran coach Lawrie Glasson to assistant manager in charge of coaching. This set the seal on a management team that was to achieve what no one had yet done at the club – make Meadowbank Thistle a footballing force in the land.

The Christie/Glasson axis would be crucial to the future playing success of the club, but so would the chairmanship of John Blacklaw. Blacklaw was an interesting and important figure at the club in his own right and his benign influence was felt for many years.

He had been a Squadron leader with Bomber Command in the RAF during the Second World War and had flown 'sorties' over enemy territory.

On one of these missions, Blacklaw's aircraft had been shot down, and he was lucky to escape relatively unscathed. If nothing else, this tough wartime background ensured that the former squadron leader would be unlikely to be daunted by any of the challenges posed even by the mysterious workings of Scottish football.

After the war, Blacklaw made use of his military contacts by joining Ferranti in Edinburgh as what was known as a 'post design services liaison officer' – essentially his job was to keep relations between the company and the Ministry of Defence running smoothly though he was also an electronics specialist. Again, this experience was to prove useful in the sometimes-fractious world of league football.

Though he had no particular track record in sport – unlike Bill Mill, Hugh Cowan, and John Bain who had all been good players before becoming administrators – Blacklaw had a passion for football as well as a flair for administration. He was used to planning ahead at Ferranti, regularly constructing and implementing five year plans; his approach to football was to be little different. It was natural therefore that Blacklaw, who was to retire from Ferranti in 1976, should be parachuted in as chairman of Meadowbank Thistle when it started its league history in 1974. Blacklaw's main role initially was to represent Ferranti's financial interests in the club. Though Ferranti never sponsored the team – despite the fears of the Scottish League – it did lend the club £1,000 in 1974 to pay for new kit and other vital equipment and it did allow its payroll to deduct contributions from fans within the company to help fund the team. As a trusted senior member of staff with unquestioned integrity, Blacklaw was the perfect choice as far as Ferranti were concerned. As events turned out, he was also a perfect choice for the football club. Within a season Blacklaw had not only balanced the books with the help of treasurer (and secretary) Bill Mill, he had managed to repay the Ferranti loan in full and still ended up with a £3,500 profit. Even during the following years when the attendances dipped and the team's league form struggled, Meadowbank never went into debt – admittedly thanks in part to some decent cup runs.

Blacklaw was also a reassuring figure as one of the public faces of the club, even if he did not come from a traditional football background. Nor, despite his reputation for tight financial controls, was Blacklaw unafraid to 'think big' on behalf of the club. For example, he put his weight behind the eventually fruitless plans to develop the swimming pool at Portobello as an alternative venue for the club.

It was perhaps Blacklaw's working relationship with Terry Christie that was to be one of his most important contributions to the future direction of Meadowbank Thistle.

In the early days of the club, the control of playing affairs had been in the hands of committee members such as Hugh Cowan and Bill Mill. Indeed, the committee had run the side for a while after the resignations of both John Bain and Alec Ness, though without conspicuous success. At this time Blacklaw had stayed in the background, his relationship with the manager less prominent.

By the time Christie was assistant manager, however, Blacklaw was taking a closer interest in the playing side and his relations with the team management a crucial part of the club. Blacklaw the former squadron leader turned liaison officer and Christie the head teacher got on well together. When Christie took temporary charge of the team, the chairman was quickly impressed by the younger man's determination and drive to succeed, even if he was clear that his teaching career came first.

Blacklaw was also the man who could ensure that the club kept to its local roots and remained a true team of Edinburgh, notwithstanding the fact that the majority of players were no longer employees at Ferranti. For Blacklaw loyalty and team spirit were essential elements of the club, and had to be maintained if the team was to achieve success on the pitch. Indeed the chairman once revealed the extent to which he saw Thistle as a 'family' club firmly entrenched in its community. 'I told our manager Terry Christie I'd always felt we should get 11 boys from Edinburgh, get somebody to train them and see what they could do.'

In any organisation, success depends on key personnel working well together, understanding each other's requirements, and instinctively bonding to form a team. So it was at Meadowbank, with Terry Christie and John Blacklaw emerging as the key men who would take the club to undreamed of heights. It was a transformation that would occur with startling speed.

The bare facts of the first years of Christie's managership gave little clue as to what was about to happen. The end of the 1980/81 season, during which Christie had taken overall control at the halfway point, proved another disappointment for the Edinburgh outfit. Thistle managed to make 13th place, one spot lower than the previous season. Without the firepower of John Jobson, who was leading scorer with twelve league goals, the results would have been far worse. The club's run in the Scottish Cup that season had already been abruptly terminated by the inglorious defeat at the hands of Buckie Thistle (Highland teams were always happy to gain the scalp of the club that robbed one of their membership of league football). Nor was the League Cup any better that season. Thistle lost their two-leg tie against Clydebank in the second round quite comfortably, their 2-1 home defeat followed by a similar scoreline away. (This was at least some improvement on the previous two seasons when Meadowbank had met Aberdeen each time in the second time. In the 1978/79 fixtures, Thistle had lost 5-0 at home and then 4-0 away, while the following year the Edinburgh side managed to restrict the Dons to just seven goals over course of the two legs, while at least managing two of their own. The consolation was that the home ties against Aberdeen attracted a thousand or more people each, while the away matches were watched by more than 6,500 – a very valuable source of income for Thistle.)

Nor was Christie's first full season in charge significantly better. The end of the 1981/82 season saw the club finishing just one place higher than the previous one, in twelfth spot, still one position worse than their 'best ever' performance of 1977. For the third time in a row, and for the last time for the club, Jobson was top scorer in the league, hitting the target 15 times. For a three month run until February 1981, the club went without a single win in the league. The season also ended on the most dismal of notes when the club managed to win just one point from its last seven games. Equally alarming – and obviously related to the continuing poor performances in the league – was the fact that average home attendances at Meadowbank Stadium had fallen steeply by 100 to just 275 a game. Seven years after joining the league, Edinburgh's third team were finding it harder than ever to make much of a mark on the football watching public of the capital.

The League Cup that year at least brought in some revenue thanks the authorities' decision to revert to the section style form of the competition, in which teams played in mini-leagues. In their five League Cup games, they were the mode of mediocre consistency. Thistle won two (oddly they won both their away games, at East Fife and Stranraer), drew two and lost one, scoring and conceding seven goals and finishing third in Section 9 on six points. Ominously, though, two of their home matches against Albion Rovers and Arbroath attracted just 250 fans each.

It was in the Scottish Cup, however, that the first signs of what Christie's Meadowbank could achieve could be glimpsed. After disposing of Arbroath and then Coldstream in the first two rounds, Thistle then travelled to meet Second Division leaders Clyde in the third round. A hard-fought 2-2 draw set up an attractive replay back at Meadowbank

Stadium which the home side eventually won 4-2 before an encouragingly-sized crowd of 700. This set up the much more exciting (and lucrative) prospect of a trip to Dens Park to play Premier League side Dundee. Christie himself had of course been on the books at Dundee for five seasons, though the former winger readily admitted he had not been good enough to get into the team at that time. Sandwiched between the win against Clyde and the tie against Dundee was a 6-1 league thrashing of Stenhousemuir, Thistle's highest league tally for one game. In this kind of form, the Edinburgh club privately hoped they could pull off a shock result against Dundee. As it turned out, Thistle ended up 3-0 losers but not before showing that the Second Division outfit had plenty of character under manager Terry Christie and more skill and organisation than their league position might suggest. Yet despite the modest cup run and the glimpses of league form, there was still nothing to give grounds for anything but a renewed feeling of pessimism among Thistles small but loyal base of fans as the 1982/83 season approached.

Perhaps it was a good omen, but Terry Christie began the new season with a promotion of his own. The Meadowbank Thistle manager was appointed headteacher of Ainslie Park School in Edinburgh, a comprehensive with around 1,000 pupils. Though football was Christie's passion, his teaching was his career and where his priorities inevitably had to remain. As he reiterated to the Daily Express's Jock MacVicar early that season: 'Football is very much a hobby really. It's difficult at times making the time to attend to the football. For example, tomorrow night is a parents' night at the school and I can't take the training at Meadowbank.' These might not have seemed encouraging words for a club that wanted to improve its league position, though they were merely a reflection of the reality of Second Division life where both players and managers needed other sources of income to survive. In any case, Christie knew – and acknowledged publicly – that he was lucky to have two men at the club who could bear the brunt of much of the workload- his assistant manager Lawrie Glasson and coach Tom McLaren. Glasson was of course a veteran of many years, one of those at the club who could recall the old days when he had played for Ferranti Thistle in the East of Scotland League. McLaren too was a hard-working and no-nonsense coach who earned the respect of the players and who knew his way around Second Division football. Together these two men worked hard behind the scenes, ensuring that Christie's vision for the team was translated into reality on the field of play. As the manager cheerfully admitted: 'They do a tremendous amount of work – without them I just couldn't do it.'

The League Cup was the start of the success that Meadowbank's management team was so eager to enjoy. For the first time in the competition, Meadowbank put together a string of good consistent performances. They managed wins against Albion Rovers, Montrose and Stranraer and drew with Stenhousemuir. Their only loss in the section was against Cowdenbeath with whom Thistle shared first spot. In the play-off Cowdenbeath ran out 3-0 winners but Christie's men had begun to put together a string of performances. These small but welcome successes were not without their costs, however. Chairman John Blacklaw bemoaned the fact that the congestion of League Cup fixtures meant that clubs such as Thistle were having to play every Wednesday evening as well as Saturday afternoon. This, said Blacklaw, meant that the club's overheads were increased without a resulting match of income from poorly attended midweek fixtures. An example given at the time was a Celtic home League Cup against Alloa which attracted for Parkhead a disappointing crowd of just 6,000. As Blacklaw pointed out with more than a little justification: ' What chance is there for clubs with less glamour than Celtic?'

For away matches it could also mean that the Thistle players would have to leave Edinburgh at around 4pm, which was during work time – and so the players would have to be compensated for loss of wages. Meanwhile the team might not arrive back at home in the city until 12.30am or 1am the next morning, hardly ideal preparation either for a player's work or for their training and match preparation. Blacklaw urged the league to consider playing all matches on Saturdays, leaving the mid-weeks free to soak up postponed games, replays and, where appropriate, European fixtures.

These complaints were part of a wider concern among clubs at the time, especially those in the Second Division. As so often, one of the major worries was about the cost of travel. The division contained 14 clubs. Each team played the other thirteen three times, 39 games in total. Twenty-six of these games were the usual home and away duels against the same club, but the remaining additional thirteen games would be a mixture of home or away fixtures. This could mean paying the same team twice at home which was fine. But it could also mean playing the same team away twice in the same season – which could put a massive burden on a small club having to travel long distances against a faraway opponent. Nor was there any financial benefit from travelling to a club that attracted a large home gate, as from February 1981 the League allowed clubs to keep their own gates.

The second, more general complaint was that the Second Division was the forgotten division, rarely if ever attracting any television or radio coverage, receiving little or no publicity from the league, and occupying ever-smaller and more obscure corners of newspaper pages. They were, they claimed, locked into a vicious circle in which they lacked resources to improve standards and thus attract more publicity – and income. They were complaints and grievances that were to remain for many years to come.

Yet despite chairman Blacklaw's genuine concerns, the signs were there at last that Meadowbank were on the verge of some kind of breakthrough in the league – which was always their top priority.

It had been a busy close season for Christie, apart from his new job as a head teacher. He had recruited a new goalkeeper Jim McQueen, from Tranent Juniors, former Berwick defender John Salton, former Hibs midfield player Mike Korotkich, ex East Fife forward George Neilson and former hearts striker David Scott. Veteran striker Mickey Lawson, who started his career back in 1971 with Stirling Albion, was signed right at the start of the league campaign and added valuable experience to the attack. These joined the nucleus of a squad whom Christie and his management team had been quietly building in the last season and a half. At the heart of this squad were; skipper Lawrie Dunn, an attacking right-back, the ever-dependable Walter Boyd who regularly chalked up 30 league appearances a year, whether in defence or midfield, defender Gordon Fraser – who had been signed as a schoolboy by Willie MacFarlane – speedy midfielder Adrian Sprott, the hard-as-nails midfielder David Conroy, the emerging defender Peter Godfrey, and the skilful goalscorer Tom Hendrie. (Christie had known 26-year-old Hendrie since the player was 12, when the teacher coached him in a schools team at Forrester High School in Edinburgh.) One veteran figure in the squad was the ever-dependable forward Roddy Georgeson, a determined player who always gave 100 per cent despite having arthritis in one hip. Another key figure who joined the club on loan was Hearts player Chris Robertson, brother of the well-known John Robertson (the former Meadowbank ballboy....) Christie showed he was prepared to make bold decisions about players. Part way through the season he let John Jobson leave for Falkirk, in a deal which saw Falkirk striker Gordon Smith moving to Meadowbank; and this despite the fact that Jobson, who had had a slow start to the season, had been the club's top league marksman for the three previous years. Another new face brought in by Christie part way through the season was Alloa defender Jim Stewart, whose partnership with Peter Godfrey at the heart of the defence ensured Thistle were far more secure at the back than in previous campaigns. (Stewart cost £3,000, by far Thistle's most expensive signing and one of only three players in the squad who had been bought.)

One figure missing from the line up that began the league season was central defender Derek Brown. Brown, who was 22, had played for Thistle for three seasons and was a dependable and very popular member of the squad. Unfortunately, the recently qualified physical education teacher, a graduate of Jordanhill College, had been unable to find work in the country. As a result Brown had looked abroad for employment and at the start of the season had signed up for work in the United Arab Emirates. It was a reminder of the unpredictability of life in the Second Division and the dilemmas that constantly faced part-time players and their managers.

Yet Christie was undaunted, even by this late loss of a key squad member, and looked ahead to the league competition this season with rare optimism. Having taken time to mould the squad into his liking, Christie was convinced that the club could achieve more than the 'respectability' it had been seeking since joining the Scottish League. A finish in the top half of the table was now the firm goal of the club. 'We are now part of the Second Division scene and have no problem keeping players. We are definitely on the way up.'

The club's start to the 1982/83 season quickly demonstrated that Christie's unconsciously prophetic words were more than just the usual public ritual optimism of any manager on the eve of battle. Win began to follow win. For once, Thistle did not mix up great results with abysmal defeats. In their first seven matches, they picked up 13 out of the available 14 points – a previously unknown run of form at the club- and won the first five. As the points steadily accumulated through September and early October, a mood of confidence began to rise in the club. Eventually, the media began to notice something odd was happening in the Second Division – Meadowbank Thistle were at the top. As the *News of the World* – who did not routinely run stories on Edinburgh's third team – put it: ' "Cinderella" Thistle are having a ball.' A few weeks later, as Thistle enjoyed a four-point leader over rivals Arbroath and Berwick Rangers, the *Daily Express* joined in the fun. Its headline ran: 'The new image'. Underneath were the unlikely words – and ones that had never appeared before in a newspaper: 'Now Meadowbank are enjoying life at the top.'

As *Express* sports writer Jock McVicar neatly put it: 'Their victory [2-1 against Arbroath] on Saturday has really made people sit up and take notice of a team that until now has been virtually forgotten in a stadium much more famous for its athletics meetings.'

By late November Thistle's position in the Second Division looked even healthier. The club that had hitherto never been out of the bottom four of the division was now entrenched at the summit, having picked up 25 points from 15 games. The side's only defeat had been against East Fife and they were unbeaten away from home, having conceded a miserly six goals in eight matches away from Edinburgh. The club's fans could have been forgiven a feeling of vertigo as they looked down at the chasing pack of the division, who were a full six points adrift. It was, as Edinburgh's *Evening News* rightly commented, an 'astonishing transformation' for a side that had performed so poorly in the league since 1974.

Everyone had their views on why and how Meadowbank had suddenly turned around their form in so dramatic a fashion. The *Evening News* praised the 'effort, enthusiasm, patience, and astute handling of the playing side by manager Terry Christie.' It also complimented the off-field contribution of chairman John Blacklaw for providing financial stability in the background.

The *Daily Express* singled out the form of the four-man Thistle midfield, in which Tom Hendrie, Walter Boyd, and Adrian Sprott – who was being linked with English First Division club Everton at the time – were all scoring valuable goals.

Manager Christie himself pointed to a number of factors in their meteoric rise up the division. These included the signing of experienced players such as Mickey Lawson, John Salton and of course Chris Robertson, plus the arrival of their talented young goalkeeper Jim McQueen – someone who could match and even surpass the achievements of Derek Gray in previous years. The other main factor, said Christie, was that his existing core of players had developed together, growing in confidence and experience with every game. Christie said: 'We have certainly made a very good start in the championship race – I think the reason is that my younger players, who are a year older now, are beginning to benefit from the more experienced hands in the side.'

He added: 'Being a part-time side we don't get together as often as we'd like but the glut of mid-week fixtures recently has helped to mould the side and improve their teamwork.'

The club had also, to be fair, had its share of luck in recent weeks, something that had been absent in previous campaigns. Against Albion Rovers, for example, Thistle had the befit of playing against opponents who lost their goalkeeper for the entire second half, enabling the Edinburgh club to squeeze out a 4-3 win. They had earlier been struggling and had been 2-1 down at half time. They were also fortunate to beat Forfar in November, a game in which the opposition had been 'all over us' according to Christie. Yet, a spectacular 25-yard free kick by Adrian Sprott minutes from full time gave Thistle a valuable 1-0. It was the kind of scrappy result that Meadowbank had simply not been achieving in previous years.

The players themselves also pointed to an increase in support for the side. Sprott, the 20-year-old Fisons clerk, said it was noticeable that more Thistle fans were travelling to away matches, which accounted in part for their superb away form. (Some wags of course insisted that the Meadowbank Stadium pitch was so far away from the fans that even home games felt like away fixtures.) Sprott pointed to the impact that such dedication from supporters can have on a side. 'When you see a bunch of supporters who have taken the trouble to travel to an away game – especially in places like Stranraer – it makes you want to play well for them.'

Not that the rise in the number of fans was likely to trouble the big Edinburgh pair, Hearts and Hibs. Even at the end of the season the average gate was still only 546 per game. Yet this was the third highest average attendance in their history – and their highest for six years – and was roughly double the previous season's dismal support. Some home league matches were now attracting 800 or 900 people, pleasingly close to the magic 1,000 mark.

Such was Meadowbank's form at this still early stage of the season, that perhaps inevitably the dreaded P-word – promotion – was on everyone's lips. Even a few weeks before the idea of Meadowbank Thistle playing in the First Division would have been unthinkable; at best, a joke. Now, however, it was looking a strong possibility. The management team of course played down the prospects of promotion in time honoured managerial fashion. 'There's a long, long way to go yet before we start talking about promotion,' one of the typical comments from the manager. Yet already the club had little choice but to consider the implications of joining the First division. The first issue, of course, was money; could the club afford the higher wage bills, transfer fees, and transport costs of higher-level football. Then there was the rented home stadium. What would First Division clubs make of the cramped changing rooms and remote playing field at Meadowbank Stadium? Publicly club secretary Bill Mill played down the concerns. 'We'll cross those bridges when we get to them,' he told inquisitive reports. But behind the scenes Thistle had held a special board meeting to discuss the next two years of the club, including most importantly what would happen if the unthinkable happened and the team made it into the First Division. The meeting must have had an almost surreal quality to it. Only a few months ago, promotion was not even a distant hope on the horizon; the question had been simply how to avoid remaining the Atlas of the Second Division – holding everyone else up. Now, to the objective observer at any rate, Meadowbank were favourites to gain promotion. The members of the board at this time were John Blacklaw, the chairman, secretary Bill Mill, the inaugural manager John Bain, Peter Glasson – father of assistant manager Lawrie Glasson – and current team boss Terry Christie.

Remarkably, the board was upbeat about the prospects for the future, even if the club did face the increased expense of playing at a higher level. Thistle continued to be run on a sound financial footing and the club was regularly receiving more income each season than it was paying out. Moreover, as the club had no capital assets – Meadowbank Stadium was rented from the council – Blacklaw had long ago decided that they needed to build up a decent cash surplus as a contingency fund. One of these contingencies was clearly playing First Division football. Without revealing too many details, Blacklaw revealed the board's careful confidence that they could cope with promotion. 'We looked at all aspects of the situation and believe we can operate without any changes for the next two years, even if things didn't work out. At the worst, we would still be all right for two years – and that's a long time in football these days.'

It was a promising sign, as far as the team were concerned, that the club looked upon potential promotion as a healthy challenge rather than a problem. Not many years before, it should be remembered, there had been rumours of clubs who mysteriously avoided promotion from the Second Division when it seemed within their grasp, therefore ensuring the club's costs did not increase. Thankfully, Meadowbank's officials had too much ambition for the club to allow them themselves to contemplate such thoughts.

As the New Year approached, Blacklaw was publicly contemplating not just promotion but winning the Second Division. 'I am always by nature a wee bit cautious but going into the New Year am reasonably optimistic about the outcome. I certainly relish the challenge facing us and am looking forward to see the championship flag flying at Meadowbank.'

The chairman also made it clear that with the club in good shape off the field, it really was now time for the team to deliver the results to match. 'Terry Christie has completed his team-building activities and now it's up to him to convert that into winning action on the field.' Blacklaw knew his man, and clearly thought that Christie would thrive on the extra pressure that such statements put on him. It was also a remarkable sign of the club's ambition and confidence considering the previous eight seasons of poor league results.

The big question for Thistle fans at the start of 1983 was; would the side feel the pressure of unfamiliar success and 'bottle' their chance of promotion? Manager Christie was realistic, predicting that their runaway lead in the first half of the season was unlikely to last; if nothing else he feared that the heavier winter pitches would slow down their 4-4-2 formation in which Hendrie and Sprott played as genuine wide men. But he was still confident his team would pick up enough points to guarantee a promotion slot. Slowly the points and milestones kept coming. On January 4 Thistle's win over Queen of the South was their 13th of the season, the most they had ever recorded in a season. Three weeks later, against Stenhousemuir, Thistle moved on to 33 points, their highest ever total. (Tom Hendrie scored a hat-trick in the 3-1 win, Thistle's first on their home ground.) With £500 of pools money awarded per each point to clubs, this was guaranteeing a profitable season for Meadowbank, irrespective of their promotion hopes.

These remarkable achievements were made even greater by the fact that Thistle had a squad of just 17 players and that two of these – David Scott and Mike Korotkich – were out with a broken leg and broken ankle respectively for much of the season.

Inevitably, the pressures did begin to have an effect on the side. Three key players – Tom Hendrie, Jim Stewart and David Conroy all picked up suspensions – though shrewdly Christie had signed the veteran midfielder Bobby Ford, whose clubs had included Dundee and most recently Dunfermline. Some stuttering performances – notably a bad defeat against Albion Rovers – increased their fans' fears that Thistle were perhaps about to blow this golden opportunity. A bad 3-0 home loss to fellow promotion hunters Arbroath seemed to underline their concerns. Already Brechin City were neck and neck with Meadowbank for the

Second Division title – were the Edinburgh side about to throw away the second promotion spot as well? Fortunately for the supporters, Terry Christie's team were not about to pass up on this opportunity. Aided by some powerful late season performances from Bobby Ford, Thistle kept picking up enough points.

The crucial game took place between Thistle and Brechin City at Glebe Park, and so much depended on the outcome. The perfect result for both teams would be a draw; Brechin would win the title, and the Edinburgh side would get the second promotion spot. A Meadowbank defeat would mean them missing out on promotion. The referee was Jim Renton (more recently club secretary at Livingston) who recently recalled what happened in the game: 'It was almost a capacity crowd at Glebe Park with both sets of players and fans somewhat apprehensive, and the game appeared to be heading for a dour draw. Then, with ten minutes to go, Dickie Campbell of Brechin scored with a deflected free kick – and the whole atmosphere of the game changed as Brechin were now due to go up with Meadowbank missing out.

'Terry Christie went ape in the away dug out at the amiable John Ritchie [Brechin's boss] and it appeared to me that they apparently had a pact that the game was meant to finish in a draw, thus ensuring both teams were promoted.

'I am sure Dick's free kick would not have gone in without the deflection but such is football. The score remained that way until Meadowbank got a penalty late into injury time from which they equalised – and both teams were promoted.' The penalty was scored by that reliable old timer, Mickey Lawson; guaranteeing him a unique place in the hearts of Thistle fans.

It was certainly an unorthodox and dramatic finale to the season, and though they had missed out on the silverware, few at Meadowbank were complaining.

A side that had never finished outside the bottom four of the Second Division had now gained elevation to the First Division. After eight years as a league side, Meadowbank Thistle had finally made their mark on Scottish football.

The plaudits to Thistle's extraordinary achievements inevitably and rightly went to Terry Christie. Though many of the players used by Willie MacFarlane had remained at the club, Christie had blended them with some experienced players at the start of the 1982/1983 – only his second full season in charge of the side. Then, as the season progressed, he had picked up other valuable players such as Chris Robertson, Jim Stewart and towards the end Bobbie Ford. These veterans had mixed well with younger stars such as Adrian Sprott. Meanwhile at the heart of the team were men such as skipper Lawrie Dunn and Walter Boyd; players whose consistency and durability marked them out as ideal club men for any manager.

Those connected to the club, however, also realised that John Blacklaw deserved much of the praise too. His planning and foresight had ensured that the club ran smoothly and was financially sound, a huge reassurance for the management team and players. Blacklaw also made sure all the players knew exactly what the wage and bonus structures were, so there could be no misunderstandings. At the same time, his aim of recruiting mostly local players helped create the family and local atmosphere the crowd thrived on. Out of 17 squad members, 15 lived in Edinburgh with one each residing in Whitburn and Grangemouth.

The promotion was also a 'family affair' in another sense. The Ferranti Company had maintained its links with its old team, and indeed some of its staff still helped to fund it. Board members John Blacklaw, Bill Mill, John Bain, and Peter Glasson were all old Ferranti hands, as was assistant manager Lawrie Glasson and unpaid 'backroom boys' Bill Robertson and Ron Galbraith. The Honorary President was the retired general manager of Ferranti in Scotland Sir John Toothill and many senior executives at the company were members of Thistle's Founder Members Club. Indeed Blacklaw went so far as to tell *Ferranti News* it was 'questionable' whether the club could have survived without the strong Ferranti connection and help. Its staff certainly rejoiced in their erstwhile team's success in the Scottish league.

Meanwhile the finances were in sound shape and the club had built up a surplus to be spent on the challenges ahead. In the 1982/83 season its turnover had been around £80,000. Of this around £20,000 came from the pools, £10,000 from the Tote, another £25,000 from the club lottery, plus some £1,000 from Ferranti staff who supported the club and £1,450 from programmes and advertising. The gate accounted for just over a tenth of the turnover, at between £8,000 and £10,000. Blacklaw was very clear with Christie about how the club's finances would dictate the players the side could have. 'If we can't afford another player we don't buy,' he said. But the chairman also knew that a football club was above all about performances and results. In earlier years, when Thistle had been wilting under complaints that they were not worthy of league status, he had told the squad: 'The only way to answer such criticism is by your deeds on the park.' Now this Thistle squad had indeed come up with an emphatic reply to all those who had questioned the club's right to be in the Scottish League.

The club had little time to waste feeling pleased with itself, however. Everyone knew that the First Division would be a major challenge for the team, even though a number of the players had experienced this level before. One of the concerns was, once again, the stadium and in particular its changing room facilities. Even before the start of the First Division campaign in 1983/84, the club was very aware that the narrow and cramped changing rooms would not be popular with visiting teams. Private complaints from teams such as Kilmarnock only added to the pressure to improve the facilities at the ground. The problem was that it was not their ground to improve but was owned by the council who had to approve – and possibly help fund – any of the work.

Meanwhile the club pointed out that they had been asked in 1974 to move to the stadium by the football authorities, and that both the Scottish league and the SFA had approved the ground for use. In other words, could there be some financial help from the authorities to improve the changing rooms? The issue rumbled on with some months, with Thistle even suggesting the use of Portacabins as a solution. Eventually work started on new facilities; but for the immediate future the cramped changing rooms remained a source of mild irritation with visiting teams.

Nor was everything well with the players in the eve of the season. A short-lived mini players' revolt from eight squad members over pay briefly soured the usually good relations between club and players. Despite a reasonable promotion bonus, the players were unhappy that their basic wage in the First Division was going to be similar to those they had in the Second, with only the appearance money increased. Eventually after some concessions, the eight singed their new contracts; but it was a reminder of how money issues could excite dissent, even among part-time players and even in the best-run clubs.

There was also a recurrence of the broken leg jinx that had settled upon Meadowbank in recent seasons. Four players had broken legs or ankles in the past three seasons; the fifth was now 22-year-old plasterer and midfield hard man David Conroy who had recently signed a new three-year contract. He unluckily broke a bone just 60 seconds into a pre-season friendly against Hibs; which was probably some kind of unfortunate record. Just as unluckily, Thistle lost the services for some weeks of a new signing John Stalker, who fell off some scaffolding at work.

Thistle set themselves a modest target for the new season. For them, survival in the First Division – even by one point – would be rated as success. John Blacklaw set a target of 18 points by the end of December and 34 by the end of the season, enough, more or less, to guarantee them staying up. Christie himself was sparing about bringing in new players, confident that his existing squad had the ability to survive at this level. His main emphasis during pre-season training and matches was to improve the squad's fitness and strength to cope with the extra speed and physical demands of the First Division. The few news faces that did arrive included another seasoned player, Colin Campbell, formerly with Hibs, and Colin Tomassi. Chris Robertson, who had been on loan from Hearts the previous season, also signed for Thistle – and ended up as the team's top scorer in the league with ten goals.

Their first match – against recently relegated Morton – showed what a tough task lay ahead of them, Thistle going down 4-1 at home. In the end, though, Thistle did survive the season, though not without a few scares on the way, and finished eleventh out of fourteen. It was a kind of success. The biggest disappointment, perhaps, was the level of attendance; and average of just 538 watched their home league matches, which was a slight fall on the previous year when they were in a lower division.

The club's real success, however, came in the League Cup; earning them not just some favourable headlines and some big scalps, but enough money to make the season a financial success. (The club was also helped by a sponsorship deal with Edinburgh company Sports Conscious who provided £2,000 worth of kit.)

The run began with a two-leg tie against Partick Thistle, another First Division side, but one expected to challenge for promotion to the Premier League that season. In the first leg at Meadowbank Stadium, the Edinburgh Thistle went a goal up within a minute thanks to Adrian Sprott, while Tom Hendrie – another regular from the Second Division days – scored a second after just 24 minutes. Though Partick pulled one back late on, the Edinburgh side went to Firhill for the second leg with a 2-1 advantage. To most people's surprise – and Partick manager Peter Cormack's disgust – Meadowbank did not just cling on but won this match to by a similar scoreline. Terry Christie described it as 'Meadowbank's best result ever' before adding: 'But then, everything we achieve is our best ever.'

The victories were a welcome lift to the side after a shaky start to the league programme. Even more importantly, they catapulted Meadowbank into Section 3 of the League Cup which contained three Premier League clubs; Dundee, St Johnstone and, best of all, Aberdeen. Financially, it could hardly have been better for Meadowbank. Though the club cheerfully admitted it had 'no chance' of winning the section, it could expect to net at least £10,000 from the six fixtures. By far the most lucrative of these was the away trip to Alex Ferguson's high-flying Aberdeen side, which contained stars such as Gordon Strachan, Willie Miller, and Jim Leighton. For Thistle, the trip to Pittodrie was the biggest game in its short history. Aberdeen, fresh from scoring 12 goals over two legs against Raith Rovers, predictably finished winners, by 4-0. However, one of Mark McGhee's two goals came late in injury time, and manager Christie was generally satisfied with his team's performances against Ferguson's team (for whom Strachan was absent injured). Indeed, Ferguson felt compelled to apologise to the crowd for the lack of entertainment as Thistle put up stiffer resistance than Raith Rovers. This important milestone in Thistle's continuing evolution also earned them a cheque for £5,300, thanks to a crowd of some 9,000. At home in the return match, before a decent crowd of 2,700, Thistle even managed a goal before losing 3-1. The results against Dundee were far better, a narrow defeat at home and a very creditable 1-1 draw away. The best performances in the League Cup, however, came against St Johnstone; as Thistle drew at home and managed a 2-1 win away in Perth thanks to goals from Gordon Smith and Tom Hendrie. Financially, the series of high-profile games made Thistle secure for the season.

Another lucrative cup run came in just one round of the FA Cup when the Edinburgh club took on Premier League side St Mirren, and held them to two draws, before finally losing 2-1 in the second replay, back at Meadowbank Stadium (and this only after the home side had taken the lead.) Most observers agreed that Thistle were unlucky not to have won the first game, which ended 0-0 and was one of the most exciting goalless draws the club ever played in. But by this time the physical demands of their higher status had begun to hit Meadowbank hard – they were barely able to muster eleven fit players for the cup-ties from their small squad. They were also hit by more unusual problems; regular goalie Jim McQueen had recently joined the fire service and was unavailable for the second replay because of his work. Instead they had to field 20-year-old Ricky Clarkson, who usually played for Easthouses Links United in the Lothians Amateur league.

Those, however, were the highlights of a season in which the club –

admittedly hit by those injuries – limped painfully towards safety. Such was the concern that they might drop down immediately to the Second Division, that late in the season chairman John Blacklaw offered the players extra win and points bonuses. Terry Christie meanwhile brought in psychologist Gerry Rooney to help both he and the players cope with the pressures of life in the division and to improve their mental preparation. The moves seemed to do the trick, and Thistle clung on to First Division status by a handful of points and with two games to go.

If Meadowbank fans feared that the results of the 1983/84 season had been a sign about the difficulties of staying in the middle division, then they were soon justified when the 1984/85 campaign began. Once again the club was aiming for 34 points and near-certain survival. Before long that looked an optimistic total as the still small Meadowbank squad struggled to show consistent form in the league. It was all the more frustrating, therefore, that the same squad showed they could raise themselves for big cup games. In the 1984/85 Scottish Cup Meadowbank did well enough, beating Partick Thistle 4-2, before losing 2-0 at home to Motherwell in the next round. However, it was in the league Cup (now called the Skol League Cup) that the Edinburgh side showed their mettle again. An impressive 2-1 against Morton saw Thistle face their local 'rivals' Hibs in round three at Easter Road. Few gave the First Division side much hope; fewer still when they shipped a goal in under 30 minutes to Ralph Callahan. But an equaliser by the resourceful Gordon Smith set up extra time, and veteran forward Mickey Lawson slotted home the winner to the astonishment of the crowd; it was a goal to rival Lawson's equaliser against Brechin to gain promotion two seasons earlier and one of the sweetest of his 188 senior goals. Hibs manager described his side's performance an 'absolute disgrace' but Terry Christie could hardly disguise his delight at their form, especially in the last 30 minutes. 'We roasted them in extra time,' he declared. The hero of the hour Lawson, meanwhile, described what the result meant to the players. 'I've always thought we would never get any recognition until we beat either Hearts or Hibs in a major competition. Well – now we've done it!'

The run had already netted Thistle £6,000 and there was more to come. A win against St Johnstone in the quarter-final set up the dream fixture of a semi-final with Premier League giants Rangers. After the previous year's games against Aberdeen, it was another step forward for Meadowbank. The results, too, were an improvement; Thistle managed to scrape a 1-1 draw at 'home' (the tie was played at Tynecastle for crowd control reasons) before losing 4-0 before 13,000 fans at Ibrox.

The experience proved to be one of the last good memories of that season. Adrian Sprott, top scorer with 14 league strikes, and new signing Alan Lawrence helped keep the Edinburgh side with a chance of survival with some valuable goals. The team even put together an impressive, almost desperate run of five successive away wins at the end of the season. But it was, as they say so often in sport, too little and too late. Thistle came 13th out of 14 in the division and headed back to the Second Division; it was little consolation that their 32 points were the highest total a First Division team had recorded and still been relegated.

Various reasons were put forward for Meadowbank's demise, though in truth they had performed only marginally worse than last season in a very competitive division. Many observers blamed the League Cup run, which may have raised money for Thistle, but had diverted attention from the primary goal of gaining league points and also worn down an already small squad. Manager Christie appeared to agree about the impact of that cup run. 'We were...totally distracted from the business of gathering points – and that probably cost us our First Division place.'

The sale of key defender Peter Godfrey to St Mirren in January had probably not helped matters either – the first player the manager had sold at the club – though Christie had recruited centre half Grant Tierney from Cowdenbeath as a replacement.

At least Thistle knew what to expect when they once more faced Second Division football at the start of the 1985/86 season. After all, it was a division they had spent nearly ten years in before their unexpected elevation. For some players, such as Adrian Sprott, the thought of returning to the lower rung was too much to bear, and the striker asked for a transfer. Generally, however the team spirit was good, with Christie and his players determined to make it straight back up to the middle division. There was some welcome good news off the field, meanwhile, as the Meadowbank Stadium finally got the new changing rooms that home and visiting players alike had been demanding. The new rooms, opened soon after the start of the new season, meant that players no longer had to share midweek facilities with squash players, weight-lifters and a whole range of other sports people. They had been installed after lengthy negotiations with the owners of the stadium – the local council – and at a cost to the club of more than £20,000. Most of this money had come from the sale of Godfrey for £30,000, though the club also hoped for a contribution from the Football Grounds Improvement Trust. (Curiously, the district council did not help fund the project even though it was their arena that was being improved.) Though one could argue that this money could have been spent on new players that were not the Thistle style. The ever-frugal John Blacklaw encouraged Christie to bring in either junior players or those from senior clubs who had been given free transfers. Darren Jackson, a teenage striker signed from Melbourne Thistle, and a player who was about to make a brief but big impact at the club, was an example of how successful this policy could be. In any case, the development of the changing rooms had also shown the club was still ambitious to succeed at a higher level; the poor facilities at Meadowbank had been a source of irritation between the club and some First Division visitors.

Thistle did not want to repeat their costly error of last season and lose focus on gaining points and promotion; so it was perhaps no great surprise or disappointment when they made early exits from both major cup competitions. In the League Cup Thistle were beaten 3-2 at home by Forfar Athletic. More embarrassingly, they departed from the Scottish Cup in the second round after drawing with non-league Nairn County away then losing 2-1 at home. Just for once, the cup giant killers were being slain themselves.

After a shaky start, however, in which they lost three of their first four games, Thistle found their feet in the league and began to press their claims for promotion straight back up. In part this was due to the enthusiasm and skill of their two young strikers, Alan Lawrence and their new star Darren Jackson; the move of the ever-dependable Walter Boyd to sweeper also helped shore up the defence. It was agonisingly close; but in the end Meadowbank left themselves too much to do and they finished in third place, one away from the two promotion spots.

The third spot finish, though disappointing, did at least confirm to the club that they were certainly now among the better teams in the Second Division, and they were now confident that the following season would be their year. The high spot had been the performances and goals of Lawrence and Jackson who ended the season as joint top scorers with 17 league goals apiece. The speed and skill of Jackson in particular was already beginning to attract attention from bigger clubs. Christie considered Jackson to be the best player in the division; he also knew it would be hard for him to keep him at the club.

The 1986/87 season was the year that Meadowbank truly came of age as a major force in Scottish football. The experience and shrewdness of Terry Christie as manager was recognised as a tremendous asset and was making its mark on the field. Meanwhile the policy of recruiting young talent was reaping the benefits not just on the pitch but in the bank balance as well. Predictably the talent scouts had come in for Darren Jackson, and the club could not stand in the way of his ambition – or the £40,000 fee – when he signed for English side Newcastle. (The club collected another £20,000 when Jackson completed 20 first team games for the Magpies.) Soon Alan Lawrence, the other joint scorer was on his way as well, signed up by Dundee. But with the £90,000 raised by Thistle that season they could attract new players, maintain financial security – and even buy one or two players of their own. The biggest signing was Victor Kasule – the only black player in Scottish league football at the time – from Albion Rovers for £32,000, then the biggest transfer fee between two Second Division sides. The reasoning by Christie and chairman John Blacklaw was simple. They could hardly stand in the way of ambitious youngsters such as Jackson or Lawrence, and nor did they want to. Yet by shrewd recruitment they could pick up veteran or 'discarded' players who could perform a reliable role for the team. One of these was former Hibs and Aberdeen striker John McGachie who in 1986/87 became Thistle's Player of the Year and scored 21 league goals – still a club record. Other experienced recruits in the squad included Ralph Callachan, Donald Park, and veteran goalie Murray McDermott. Christie suspected that by recruiting such proven quality he could not just gain promotion – but this time stay up in the First Division.

Certainly the League Cup was to be no distraction from those aims this season; a 4-1 defeat by Stirling Albion saw them crashing out in round one. The Scottish Cup saw Thistle fare rather better; a fourth round tie with Dundee went to two replays before the Dens Park side finally came out on top. These games were especially lucrative for the Edinburgh club; not only from the gate receipts but from the performance of Alan Lawrence whose skills in these games persuaded the Taysiders to buy him before the end of the season.

The last time Thistle had gained promotion, manager Christie had himself been promoted as head teacher of Ainslie Park High School. It was a good omen, therefore, when in the run-up to the end of the 1986/87 season Christie swapped jobs again, this time taking up the post of head at Musselburgh Grammar School. By this time Meadowbank were at the top of the division, and in line not just to gain promotion but to win the title as well. Fortunately for Thistle's fans, there was to be no repeat of the previous season's near miss. Unlike in previous seasons, the squad had suffered no major injury problems and no fewer than five of the team had played in all 39 league games; Graeme Armstrong (their dead ball specialist), the reliable Walter Boyd, Tom Hendrie, John McGachie and Dave Roseburgh. Such consistency and durability had its effect. Meadowbank duly clinched both promotion and the title, with Raith Rovers squeezing in ahead of Ayr United and Stirling Albion. (A particular highlight of the season – and one that Terry Christie remembers as one of his best at Thistle – was the team's 5-1 league thrashing of St Johnstone at Perth.) For Thistle it was their first major silverware since joining the league and a triumphant moment for all at the club, but chairman John Blacklaw and manager Terry Christie in particular. Together, this pair had forged a close alliance in which on field and off field policies worked with each other. Having witnessed the euphoria and then the deflation of promotion and then relegation, it was a management team hardened by experience and determined to do better. Now the Christie/Blacklaw partnership had got Meadowbank back once more into the pressure cooker of the First Division. An obvious question on supporters' lips was: could they stay there this time?

Just as important, though, was another query; for how long could the successful Christie/Blacklaw partnership remain intact?

6

Dissenting Voices

OR THE FANS AND PLAYERS of Meadowbank Thistle, the end of the 1986/87 season marked one of the highlights in the club's history; it might not be too far-fetched to call it a mini-golden era. They had just been promoted for the second time to the First Division; they had a settled squad and manager, and a well-run administration, which ensured the club had money in the bank. The club was now confident that it could handle the increased pressures of life in a higher division. There were few clouds on the horizon in that summer of 1987.

The feeling of optimism that surrounded Thistle lasted well into the 1987/88 season. (Off the field, there was also the happy news that John Bain, Meadowbank Thistle's first manager, had been awarded the British Empire Medal in the New Year's Honours list.) For the first time the Edinburgh side were not seen as bit players in the middle division, but as a competent, competitive team that was well able to hold its own against the opposition. For the second season in a row, John McGachie was top league scorer, this time with 14 goals – a decent performance against tougher defences. The core of the team still included players such as goalie Jim McQueen, dead ball specialist Graeme Armstrong and the seemingly indestructible Walter Boyd. They proved a hard team to beat in the league.

Once more, they failed to make any real impression in either major cup competition. Though they beat Hamilton Academicals 1-0 at home – after extra time – in the second round they were comfortably defeated 3-0 at home to Dundee in the next; though a useful crowd of nearly 3,000 turned out to watch the visitors. In the Scottish Cup the Accies had their revenge, beating Thistle 2-0 at home.

Instead, it was in the league that Thistle were to find their real successes of the season, both on the pitch and on the terrace. In 1986/87 the attendances at Meadowbank Stadium had been at their lowest since 1982, despite the prospect of winning promotion and ultimately the championship. The average home gate had been just 411 and showed just how hard it was to attract regular support even when the side was performing well. However, the arrival once more of First Division football saw this figure leap dramatically to 734 in 1987/88, the highest yet in Thistle's history. On the field, the news was just as good. A consistent run right through to the end of the season meant that Thistle were left facing a truly remarkable prospect – that of promotion to the Premier Division. To have done so would have emulated the recent feat of Dunfermline, who won the Second Division title in 1985/86 and were runners-up in the First Division the following year and won promotion. Indeed, at the start of the 1987/88 campaign manager Christie believed that if the club could afford three or four more quality players – to give the squad added depth – then they really could 'do a Dunfermline'.

However, the task of instant promotion was made doubly difficult for Thistle because of some re-organisation of the league. The Scottish League had agreed to change the size of the Premier League and also the promotion and relegation rules. These changes were to take place over a couple of seasons and 1987/88 was part of the transition period. They meant that while three teams would be relegated from the Premier Division in 1987/88, only one team would be promoted from the First Division. (The aim was to get two lower divisions of 14 teams each, with 10 in the top league, from whom one team just one team would be promoted each season and from which just one would be relegated.)

The outcome was that Thistle needed to win the First Division title that year to make the jump up to join Celtic, Rangers, Aberdeen et al. As it was they managed second spot – and so missed promotion solely because of the re-structuring.

It was of course an agonising way to miss out on what would have been a true fairytale event in Scottish football; a works team making it into the top flight of Scottish football so quickly; from zero to hero inside fifteen years.

Arguably, though, it was a hidden blessing that Meadowbank Thistle did not make it to the Premier Division. On Christie's own admission the squad was not yet strong enough to cope with the consistently higher demands. Dunfermline, themselves so recently a Second Division team, certainly found it hard to survive in the top division. Then there was the question of the ground. Regular home matches against Rangers and Celtic would have, at the very least, caused disquiet among the authorities who had to police the crowds. The extra burdens that membership of the Premier Division would have brought may well have provoked convulsions and disharmony within the club, if officials had differed over which direction to take it.

Yet if anyone thought that remaining in the First Division was the easy option for Meadowbank Thistle, then subsequent events were to prove them terribly wrong. During the 1980's the club hierarchy had remained pretty much unchanged. Chairman John Blacklaw, though no longer a young man, was still in overall charge while the long-serving treasurer and secretary Bill Mill was still in his two posts. One of the old guard, Peter Glasson, had died in 1987; but his place on the board of directors and management committee had been taken two years later by his son Lawrie, the former coach and assistant manager. Few men had served Ferranti and then Meadowbank as loyally as Lawrie Glasson. On the team side, Christie was approaching the end of his first decade in charge, and was also on the board of directors. Apart from the usual squabbles that occur in any football club, the club's administrative hierarchy essentially agreed on the direction of the club and team policy. Indeed, many other league clubs looked at Meadowbank with something approaching envy. Here was a club that was harmonious, well-run and in profit. What was more, it was one of the very few part-time clubs that was able to hold its own in the First Division. By any objective criteria, it was an astonishing achievement for a football team that had, as the newspapers liked to put it, 'come from nowhere'. Yet Meadowbank's reputation as a harmonious club with a family atmosphere was not destined to last much longer. Soon hard questions would be asked about the direction and ambition of this unfashionable but happy little football club. The resulting divisions would split the club in two. Meadowbank had never in its short history suffered from the constant behind-the-scenes bickering that had marred many league football clubs. Soon it was to find out what it was like to make headlines off as well as on the pitch; it would not be a pleasant experience.

After Thistle's extraordinary performance in coming second in their first season back in the First Division, reality set in and life among the bigger clubs became harder. Most of their opponents in the higher league were full-time professional outfits, unlike part-time Thistle. As part-timers, the squad members were not able to train as often as other players at other clubs. They also had the important distraction of their day jobs, through which they earned a living. This was also true of the manager Terry Christie, who was head teacher at Musselburgh Grammar School and whose first loyalty – inevitably – had to be to his teaching career. On most Saturday mornings, Christie could be found refereeing schools team football matches, before hurrying off to catch up with the Thistle squad either at Meadowbank or on the away coach. The financial rewards for both players and coaching staff at Thistle were not great either. For example, Christie earned the princely sum of £1,442 before tax during the

1982/83 season, the year that Thistle were promoted for the first time. In 1987/88, the year when Meadowbank so narrowly and unluckily missed out on elevation to the Premier division, the manager had grossed £1,978. This rose to £5,000 by 1992, roughly one quarter of the average salary for First Division managers (he was only one of two part-time team bosses in the division that year). No one involved with Meadowbank, whether player or manager, did it for the financial gain alone but as much as anything for the love of football.

Despite their circumstances, the club neither sought nor claimed excuses for their performances in the First Division. The year after their runners-up spot, Thistle slipped to tenth place (out of 14) as the division was swelled by three teams relegated from the Premier League. Their main problem was an inability to score enough goals; top scorer that campaign was Dave Roseburgh with just six league strikes. Nor was there any consolation in the cups. In the League Cup Thistle beat Stirling Albion in round two, only to be beaten 2-0 by Hearts in the next round, admittedly before a healthy crowd of 6,800. Meanwhile in the Scottish Cup, they avenged the previous year's defeat by Hamilton Academicals, beating the Accies 2-0 before a crowd of nearly 2,000; but they went down 1-0 at home to Morton in the next round in front of a disappointing crowd of 750. This last attendance was not typical of the season, however. Average home league gates for the club increased once again in the crowds to 848. Though no one could know it at the time, this average gate was to be as good as it got; and would be the highest the club would ever achieve at the Commonwealth Stadium.

For the next couple of seasons, Meadowbank continued to perform like the team they had become – a mid-ranking First Division side half way between the bottom of the Second division and the top of the Premier Division. In 1989/90 Thistle managed a respectable seventh out of 14, though the next year saw them slipping slightly to eleventh. Goals were, as ever, a problem, though in the second of these two seasons the ever-industrious Roseburgh managed a healthy 15 league goals and was one of four players who played in all 39-league fixtures that season. Meanwhile Meadowbank, who had once enjoyed a reputation as a dangerous cup side, seemed to be losing their cutting edge in the knockout competitions. Clydebank and then Hibernian dumped Thistle out of the League Cup's second round in 1989/90 and 1990/91 respectively, though the latter side was only decided by a single goal in extra time. As for the Scottish Cup, Meadowbank seemed to have developed the unhappy habit of meeting a determined Morton side in the fourth round of the competition. Out of four seasons from 1988/89, the Greenock side knocked Thistle out of the cup at this stage no fewer than three times. In the remaining season, East Fife put the Edinburgh side out of the competition in the third round. No longer were Meadowbank enjoying the sort of cup runs that had brought them favourable headlines – and welcome money – that they had earned in previous season. It was as if the effort required to survive in the First Division meant there was little inspiration left over for a little of the old Thistle cup magic.

This was not for lack of effort; under Christie Thistle earned a reputation for hard work and organisation. In no one was this better exemplified than Graeme Armstrong. In six out of eight seasons Armstrong played in all the available league fixtures, a record only surpassed at Thistle by Walter Boyd (who managed the feat seven times), a player whose mantle as the ever-present heart of the team Armstrong – now made captain – had assumed. Of those fans who did turn up week in, week out, to watch Thistle play, few could doubt the side's determination to succeed.

The 1991/1992 season, therefore, promised to be another of those middling seasons where Meadowbank belied their part-time status and occupied their usual spot somewhere around the middle or lower reaches of the First Division. As ever, Christie prepared his squad for a demanding season, a season made harder by the fact that though the division had been cut to twelve, the number of league fixtures had risen from 39 to 44. There had been a change at Meadowbank too, though no one guessed then quite how important this change would prove to be. John Blacklaw – aware that age was catching up with him – had invited a new face to join the board of directors, someone whom the chairman hoped would bring new vigour and fresh ideas. The new director's name was W.P. Hunter, known to most people as Bill.

Bill Hunter was no stranger to Meadowbank Thistle. Since 1979 the builder and businessman had been connected with the club and given it financial backing. Hunter, from Prestonpans – the place where Sir Walter Scott researched his novel *Waverley* – became the club's first individual match sponsor in the 1983/84 season when he bankrolled Thistle's home League Cup match with Aberdeen. The cost was around £250 and was it was one of several occasions when Hunter met the costs of home games. The former bricklayer was also part of the club's official party when it went to away matches. Hunter, a Hibs fan as a youngster, had also agreed to sponsor a Hibernian home match against Motherwell in January 1984. At the time Blacklaw said: 'Bill Hunter has supported us in many ways over the years, and we are grateful for his backing again.'

Having been associated with Thistle for twelve years, however, Hunter had wanted much more direct involvement with what went on at the club. For some period, he had wished to join the board of directors at Meadowbank, a prospect that had hitherto been resisted. The manager and board director Terry Christie was one of those who had opposed Hunter joining the club in an official capacity. As Christie later explained: 'During [the 1980's and early 1990's] Bill Hunter was always on the sidelines sponsoring games but very keen to get into the club. He was a very good friend to the club and put a lot of money into it. I was the one that continually resisted Bill's attempts to get his hands on the club. Unfortunately Bill is not a team player and wanted to run the whole show.'

No one doubted Hunter's determination, nor his business experience and the fact that he had – as Christie put it – already been a 'good friend' to the club. Apart from his sponsorship of matches, he had helped with various hospitality events and also offered his services as a builder when the need arose. The problem, as some at Thistle saw it, was that the club was a close-knit family-style outfit, with many of its key personnel bonded together by links with Ferranti. To let an outsider onto the board, even one who had been as helpful as Hunter, might be to jeopardise the smooth running of the club and upset the internal dynamics of the board.

Hunter, naturally enough, saw matters rather differently. An admirer of John Blacklaw's careful stewardship of the club, and the way it had broken even despite a low fan base, Hunter nevertheless felt the club could be more ambitious. He also understood that as Blacklaw neared the end of his time as chairman – age and the demands of the job were slowly catching up with him – change was inevitable at Meadowbank. And Hunter, like many a businessman before and after him, wanted to be part of the excitement and glamour associated with a league football club.

Blacklaw had himself already realised that his tenure as chairman – which stretched back for more than a decade and a half to 1974 – could not last much longer. He was also aware that the board could perhaps do with some fresh enthusiasm and energy. Hunter was a very experienced businessman with a good network of contacts within and around Edinburgh. The businessman had also already, so to speak, put his money where his mouth was through his financial support. True, Hunter had a reputation for bluntness and was known to be a man who liked to get his own way; in this his style was very different from that of Blacklaw himself. Yet the chairman recognised that change was on its way, and that men such as Hunter represented the future of Meadowbank. Blacklaw also knew that the organisation of the club needed to be examined; technically it was owned by the Founder Members who were had helped set up the new club back in 1974 out of the old Ferranti Thistle; such an archaic structure sat uneasily with the business demands of a modern football club. Hunter would be someone who could perhaps assist in restructuring the administrative framework of the club. Therefore, and despite the reservations of Terry Christie, Bill Hunter was invited to join the board of Meadowbank Thistle in July 1991. For good or ill, life at Meadowbank Thistle was about to change.

The relationship between Terry Christie and John Blacklaw had been foundation stone upon which much of the successes of Thistle in the 1980's had been constructed. The manager was given considerable autonomy in all team matters including selection, tactics, and also recruitment; the detail of the buying and selling of players was usually discussed and authorised between Christie and Blacklaw. In return Christie knew he was under a duty to keep spending down and to ensure that the club never spent more than it could afford. This tight financial policy could, of course, restrict the development of the team and hold the club back from scaling the heights of Scottish football. But at the same time this cautious approach to money ensured that Meadowbank Thistle – that had no capital assets such as a ground of its own to sell or raise finance against – always lived to fight another day. Blacklaw was proud that under his chairmanship the club never had an overdraft and, save its first season when it paid back a £1,000 loan from Ferranti, was never in debt. Christie and Blacklaw, who had now worked together for more than ten years, knew just where each stood with this policy and how far each could take it. One accepted result of the financial constraints of the club was that they did not stand in the way of talented youngsters who they had developed and wanted to move on to bigger clubs. The sale of Darren Jackson – later a Scottish international – and Alan Lawrence were examples of this. Therefore the squad tended to consist of young prospects who were likely to be headhunted by talent scouts, old club stalwarts or veterans from other clubs who could perform a valuable service for Thistle in the twilight of their career. John McGachie was a good example of this last category. What the club really lacked was a youth or reserve team to bring on youngsters who could provide a solid (and cheap) backbone for the club in years to come. This was finally put right in 1990 when the club established a reserve team, an innovation that quickly bore fruit. Two members, Peter Cormack and Ian Little, were capped at under-18 level for Scotland. It seemed, therefore, that the Christie/Blacklaw axis was ale to evolve and come up with new ideas without losing its solidity.

It would be wrong, however, to paint life at Meadowbank before the spring of 1992 as one of unalloyed harmony. In particular, there were some tensions within the board and around the club over the attitude of secretary Bill Mill towards some of the team and their performances. Mill was of course a former player with Ferranti Thistle and besides being an administrator for many years – in fact since the 1960's – he knew a thing or two about the game. Unfortunately, he could also be a little over-exuberant when it came to expressing his views about individual performances in public. This led to the slightly somewhat unusual spectacle of Mill shouting criticism at his own team's players (some who heard it described it as 'abuse') from the directors' box during away matches. As a result, there had been once or two occasions on which John Blacklaw had asked Mill not to attend away fixtures so as to avoid embarrassment to the club. Even worse, from the point of morale, Terry Christie had sometimes felt it necessary to apologise to the individual players concerned for the criticism they had received on the field from the veteran club secretary and treasurer. This situation reached its peak – or rather its low point – when Christie signed his own son Max from Hearts in August 1991 for £30,000. Max Christie was picked for the Scotland under-21 side but this clearly did not impress Bill Mill. According to witnesses the club secretary 'regularly and loudly scream[ed] abuse' at Christie junior during away games. So unsettling was this for the young player's form that Christie senior decided to sell his son to Dundee just nine months later for the same fee (though the deal lost the club some money in administrative the process, something that would be cited against the manager later).

Quite what lay behind Bill Mill's extraordinary behaviour was unclear; unless it was simply a symptom of his frustration with the manager that he was unwilling to take up directly with Christie himself or with chairman John Blacklaw. But the unhappy feeling it caused was a foretaste of some of the bitterness to come at Meadowbank Thistle.

One of the immediate causes of the whirlwind that was about to rip through Meadowbank's usual genteel tranquillity was ostensibly a dispute over the structure of the club. As we have seen, the club was effectively owned by the Founder Members, of whom there were some 58 left. After joining the board, Bill Hunter had been instructed to find a new way of administering the club; to consider the possibility of forming a new constitution more in keeping with late 20th century business practices. Hunter favoured establishing a limited company with a share issue; the existing Founder Members would each be allocated a number of shares. The businessman, however, feared that Christie – a board member as well as manager – was opposed to these changes. In other words, Bill Hunter saw Terry Christie as an obstacle to the modernisation of Meadowbank Thistle. Christie was later to deny this charge; he claimed he considered the idea of a limited company – with the consent of the Founder Members – as a 'sensible way ahead'. His argument, he insisted, was over how this company would be structured – and who would be the main beneficiary. Christie said he was 'opposed to the club becoming a play thing of a small businessman for a pittance and believes that if the Club does become a limited company it must do so in a way that prevents this happening.' The director and manager's fears were clear; he feared Hunter was after nothing other than the control of the football club.

Hunter, meanwhile, was equally adamant that the real problem was the board's – or at least Terry Christie's – opposition to change and that the club hade to move forward with or without Christie's support. Slowly, and unknown as yet to the outside world, the battle lines were now being drawn up for the looming struggle ahead. On one side of the divide was Terry Christie and his long-standing friend and club colleague Lawrie Glasson. Ranged against them were Bill Hunter and, unsurprisingly given his views of the footballing ability of Christie's son and other members of the team, secretary Bill Mill. Joining this pair was another new member of the board, Dr Malcolm Morrison, who had been the (unpaid) club physician for four years. In the middle and trying – as was his nature – to keep the peace was John Blacklaw. When the battle finally began, however, it was not ostensibly about the structure or organisation of the club, but over a much narrower and clearer issue; should Terry Christie remain as manager?

There was no doubt that the 1991/92 season was proving to be another mediocre one for Meadowbank Thistle. In the previous year the club had finished 11th out of 14; this time round, with only 12 teams in the division, a similar level of performance could spell disaster. Once again, though, the team was still hovering dangerously close to the relegation zone. Once again also, one of the problems was that the team was finding it hard to hit the back of the net. Dave Roseburgh would, for the second season in a row, be the club's top scorer in the league but his total was a modest eight goals. Roseburgh, skipper Graeme Armstrong and the evergreen goalie Jim McQueen were once more the mainstays of the team, but the squad was finding it hard to display much inspiration and more importantly to win many games. The club was soon dumped out of the League Cup, losing 2-0 at home to St Johnstone; inevitably, Morton saw them off in the FA Cup. Attendances, too, were falling at Meadowbank Stadium, dropping to an average of under 600 per home game – close to their old Second Division levels. To the football world, this was business as usual for Meadowbank Thistle, now accepted as a part-time team that consistently punched above its weight, but one which had to work hard to so. Inside certain parts of the club, however, the middling results were regarded as a symptom of a wider malaise. For the disgruntled, manager Terry Christie was not just opposed to modernisation of the club's structures; he was also presiding over a squad of players who were failing to perform, who lacked spark and who were struggling to entertain a dwindling fan base.

As Christmas came and went, and results continued to disappoint, the levels of anger and frustration in sections of the boardroom began to build up. Finally, at a meeting of the board on Monday 9 March, the frustrations erupted. Veteran official Bill Mill proposed the football equivalent of dropping a nuclear bomb. His proposal to the meeting was simple but deadly: a motion of no confidence in the manager Terry Christie.

Though the person who proposed the motion was Mill, there was little doubt among anyone present that it had the full backing – not to mention prior knowledge –of Bill Hunter. There were a number of reasons given, the most immediate being that Meadowbank had won just a handful of games that year and were facing a struggle to avoid relegation. This, however, was not the only reason cited by Bill Mill. He and Bill Hunter felt that the team under Christie lacked direction and purpose; it played unattractive football that was not likely to boost the club's already poor (and dwindling) attendances; and there was no proper youth policy to plan for the future. Mill and Hunter were also concerned at the way – as they saw it – that Christie conducted the buying and selling of players at the club with little or no reference to any other board members. Overall they felt that the team was crying out for fresh ideas and a 'fresh approach', and that after 12 years in charge it was time for Christie to step aside and let someone else take control.

After the tensions of recent months, it perhaps came as no great surprise to Terry Christie, and his friend Lawrie Glasson, to learn that Bill Mill and Bill Hunter were keen to see the removal of the manager. But it still came as a shock to hear the motion of no confidence and the reasons given to support it. The issue was of course greatly complicated by the fact that Christie had a dual role both as manager and board director. To he and Glasson at least it was clear that this vote was about far more than who was to manage the football team; but was instead about the direction and quite possibly the future control of the entire football club. Whatever the outcome of the impending vote, everyone at the meeting knew then that life at Meadowbank Thistle would never be the same again.

Present at the meeting were Hunter and Mill, Dr Malcolm Morrison, Terry Christie, Lawrie Glasson and, of course, the chairman John Blacklaw. One can only imagine what the ageing chairman thought of this extraordinary dispute emerging before his eyes. Since 1974, he had been in overall charge of this club, and had built up an enviable reputation for having a well-run solvent club that somehow managed to keep a wholesome, family and largely rancour-free atmosphere. For the last twelve years as well Blacklaw had forged a close working relationship with a manager who had taken the side from the foot of the Second Division to a fixture of the First Division and Scottish football's best-performing part-time team. Both achievements were now in peril. The chairman's natural inclination was to seek a compromise, and this was what he now tried to do – before the divisive issue was forced to a vote. Blacklaw proposed that the motion could be amended to allow that Christie remained as manager until the end of the season when he would 'retire' – but still remain on the board. This, apparently, was not acceptable to Christie and Glasson; with the season's end just two months away it scarcely changed the thrust of the original motion. So the chairman tried again. This time the amendment would allow for Christie to remain in charge until the end of the season; and that if Meadowbank avoided relegation, then he would continue in the job. This proposal was rejected by Hunter and Mill; understandably, as they were not arguing just about the team's performance this season but its recent past and, more importantly, its direction in the future. Blacklaw realised it was impossible to bridge the gap between the two opposing factions and the board meeting moved to a vote on the motion of no confidence. Two votes in favour of the censure – which if carried would of inevitably force the departure of Christie – came from the proposer of the motion Mill, plus Hunter. Added to these was the vote of Dr Morrison, who clearly shared the two men's disdain for Terry Christie's continuing presence as manager. Ranged against them, equally predictably, were Christie himself and Glasson, who had once been assistant manager to Christie and with whom he shared a friendship as well as a good working relationship. This made the voting 3-2 in favour of the motion. But there was still one person to vote – John Blacklaw.

His was a difficult situation. For the first time over such a major issue he was being forced to choose a course of action that would inevitably cause deep and possibly disastrous rifts within the club. If he voted with Bill Hunter and Bill Mill, then he knew that the club would not just lose Christie as a manager, but almost certainly as a director too. It was also likely that Glasson would quit with Christie. Meanwhile Bill Hunter and Bill Mill would be effectively left with the power to dictate changes at the club. On the other hand, if Blacklaw voted against Bill Hunter, he would be going against the man whom he had invited onto the board less than a year before; and would risk losing a new and powerful ally on the board. Abstention would simply produce the same result as voting with Hunter and Mill. The former RAF man had always known when it was necessary to make a decision, and did not shirk his responsibilities now. With a heavy heart, John Blacklaw made his mind up and voted – with Christie and Glasson against the motion.

The immediate significance of the vote was that the motion was not carried and therefore Christie remained as manager of Meadowbank Thistle. The immediate result of the tied vote was that the three who had backed the censure motion – Hunter, Mill and Morrison – all immediately resigned; as they later explained their situation appeared 'untenable' and it seemed the 'honourable' thing to do. On the face of it, this was a clear-cut victory for the Christie/Glasson 'faction' – if it could be described as such – and a clear defeat for Bill Hunter. But it was to become clear that very little about this increasingly bitter affair ever stayed that simple.

Within a matter of a day or two, the (apparently) losing side in the no confidence affair had begun to have second thoughts. Bill Mill and Bill Hunter in particular had, they later revealed, now had a chance to study the club's Constitution in more detail and to take legal advice on the matter. In particular, they had examined Article 5 of the document, which covered voting issues. (It was clear that they had not been aware of the possible importance of this article before the votes were cast on Monday; presumably, they had assumed Blacklaw would either abstain or vote for them.)

From this, they deduced that the chairman – John Blacklaw – could only use his casting vote when the votes were tied; and that as the voting had stood at 3-2, Blacklaw had had no right to vote in Monday's meeting. The situation, they considered, was now turned on its head – and the no confidence motion against Terry Christie had therefore won the day. As a result, it was down to John Blacklaw to enforce the will of the board and accept Christie's resignation – or effectively to sack him. Moreover, the trio had withdrawn in writing their resignations from the board/management committee. All of this was now dumped on the chairman to deal with. As far as John Blacklaw was concerned, an unfortunate situation had suddenly and dramatically got very much worse.

The Hunter faction became increasingly insistent that they had won the vote against Terry Christie and that he should be made to leave the club. Blacklaw, who had hoped that the bitter saga had ended with the vote, bore the brunt of the pressure to act – and act fast.

Meanwhile the whole saga had got into the public domain and unsurprisingly was being lapped up by the newspapers. Hunter and Mill blamed Christie for using his 'media contacts' to whip up favourable commentary on his side. The headlines were certainly sympathetic to Christie's cause. A commentary piece by Mike Aitken in *The Scotsman* had the headline: 'Meadowbank miracle man deserves better'. Another in the *Evening News* ran: 'Terry's just a miracle'. It was small wonder that Hunter and Mill resented the press coverage the case was getting; and so they made quickly for the moral high ground. They later wrote: 'We who oppose Mr Christie have deliberately chosen not to become involved in a public dispute in the newspapers as we feel the entire matter is Club business which is best discussed in the boardroom and with the Founder Members.'

The story though was about to get even more public – and even more dramatic. On 18th March Jardines, a firm of solicitors representing Bill Hunter wrote a letter to Meadowbank Thistle marked for the attention of John Blacklaw. It was delivered by hand, adding to the sense of drama. The letter explained Hunter's unhappiness with recent events at the club and in particular pointed out that the no confidence vote had been won 3-2 by Hunter, Mill and Dr Morrison. It stated: 'We are advised by our client that despite the clear decision in terms of the constitution, the then Chairman decided to use a casting vote to prevent the Motion being carried. It is clearly our view that on the information, as advised, the Motion of No Confidence in the Manager, Mr Terry Christie, was carried out.'

The letter added: 'Our client is clear in his concept of the damages that he has sustained and we are to advise him separately in that capacity.'

The tone and the content of the letter had a profound effect on John Blacklaw. An intelligent man, he could not have failed to pick up on the description of himself at the fateful meeting as the 'then chairman'; nor that the letter was simply addressed to 'J. Blacklaw Esq.', with no mention of his position as chairman. Even worse, for the first time it seemed that Hunter was prepared to sue Meadowbank Thistle for the damages he had suffered as a result of the whole episode. According to some who were close to Blacklaw at the time, this was the moment at which the wartime veteran decided he could not stand any more of the aggravation. The next day, the 19th March, the chairman apparently declared himself 'persuaded' that he should not have voted at that board meeting; and that the motion of no confidence had been passed. This of course meant only one thing – that the manager had to go.

Now events took an even murkier term. According to Bill Hunter and Bill Mill, John Blacklaw released a statement to the media informing them that Terry Christie had been removed as manager – without first informing the manager himself. This version of events (which certainly seemed unusual behaviour for the always courteous John Blacklaw) was disputed by Terry Christie and Lawrie Glasson. They insisted that the statement had been released by Bill Hunter to the *Evening News* – without the approval of chairman John Blacklaw. Certainly that was the version accepted by at least some sections of the media itself; referring to these events a few weeks later Hugh Mckinlay wrote in the *Herald*: 'The local press was informed by Mr Hunter that Christie had resigned.'

At least everyone agreed on one thing; the first Terry Christie knew that he had been dismissed, as manager was when a local journalist rang him for his reaction to the news. If Blacklaw, Hunter, or whoever had issued that statement thought that this would end the uncertainty, they were to be sadly disappointed. If anything, the intrigue and uncertainty only got worse. On hearing the news of his apparent resignation, Christie reacted with the news that he would fight any attempt to sack him with an immediate interim interdict.

That same evening members of the board gathered at a pre-arranged meeting to discuss a 'compromise' although it was by now fairly clear that a compromise was just about the last thing on most people's minds. Christie informed the meeting that he would not, as suggested, step down from the board in order to keep his place as team manager. Hunter told the manager that he would use all his resources to get him sacked and that declared: 'Headmaster or no headmaster I'm going to employ guards to keep you out of the stadium'. Rather than finding a compromise, it seemed the new meeting was simply polarising the factions even more strongly.

That evening, though, there was a development that promised a possible end to the immediate wrangling. Dr Morrison telephoned Christie to inform him he was tendering his resignation from the board. According to the manager, Morrison said he 'wanted no more to do with the affairs of Meadowbank Thistle'. According to a later account by Bill Hunter and Bill Mill, Morrison had been unhappy at the ethics of being a member of the medical profession stuck in the middle of a messy legal wrangle. In any case, Morrison had been part of the faction that wanted Christie sacked. His resignation meant that the board was now split evenly 2-2 over the issue, with Blacklaw (indisputably) having the power to cast his vote either way.

On the 20th of March, therefore Christie informed John Blacklaw that his interdict was no longer necessary as Morrison's resignation had swung power back into the hands of the chairman. The chairman's relief was short-lived however; Hunter still insisted he would have Christie barred from the ground.

And so, that same day, one of the more unusual legal actions in Scottish football history took place. Terry Christie's lawyers pleaded before the judge Lord Coulsfield that the manager of Meadowbank Thistle should not be removed, that he should be allowed into the club's stadium and should be permitted to run the team's affairs without interference. The judge granted the interdict. The club's constitution was an informal document and one that had been ignored for some time; and that as chairman John Blacklaw had for years been involved in key decisions affecting the club. His lordship added that as everyone at the meeting on 9 March had at that time believed the chairman could vote, then the decision stood.

There was of course the chance for a re-run of no confidence vote, but now that Malcolm Morrison had resigned there seemed little chance of this. The club's manager had managed to keep his job – with the help of the courts. But the position of the club could scarcely have been more unhappy or damaging. The good name of Meadowbank Thistle – once regarded as being one of the friendliest clubs in Scotland – was being dragged through the dirt. In less than two weeks, Meadowbank Thistle had gone from having a well-run administration to a chaotic shambles in which factions on the board of directors were in open warfare. Watching all this was a disconsolate John Blacklaw, who saw so much of his hard work of the last two decades being tarnished by two weeks of mayhem. He had already told friends he was 'devastated' by recent events at Meadowbank. It should have come as little surprise therefore when he announced his intention to resign as chairman.

Blacklaw was eventually persuaded to remain, temporarily, in nominal charge of the board. Perhaps stung by the decision of John Blacklaw to resign in this way – after 18 dignified years at the helm of the club – the two rival factions had agreed to preserve the status quo until the end of the season. At that time the Founders Members would be given a chance to vote on a new board or management committee, and this would effectively decide the outcome of the power struggle. For a while, then, Blacklaw remained in charge at Meadowbank. But by now he was thoroughly despondent. Back in November, the veteran chairman had apparently already decided that he would step down as chairman at the end of the current season. Age was catching up with him, and he had done his best to bring new blood onto the board. Alas the only blood to be seen at present was that which was all over the carpet after the boardroom battles of recent weeks. It was not the way the former RAF squadron leader wanted to end his years of service to his company and then football club.

Nor was there any sense of truce between the warring factions. Instead other elements waded into the argument, most, it has to be said, on the side of Terry Christie. Though it may have been easy to forget, the football season was still in full spate and Meadowbank had a relegation battle to survive. One group who had not thankfully forgotten this were the Thistle players, who veered between bemusement and anger as they watched the club's senior personalities tear each other to pieces in public. Graeme Armstrong, the club's veteran and highly respected captain, told the media that they supported their manager 'totally' and said that the squad had suffered in their preparation for vital games because of the dispute. 'The younger players in particular were affected by all the speculation,' he said. The skipper then made some shrewd observations about the way Thistle had traditionally operated. 'One of the strengths of the club has been the relationship between the players and the directors. But if they had got rid of Terry like that, it would have been difficult to live with.'

Another veteran, Dave Roseburgh, the season's top scorer, was more blunt. 'The players are sickened by the whole thing. If Bill Hunter was going to do anything, it should have been at the end of the season. I am a Terry Christie admirer, and the fact that he has not just walked away and told them to stuff it shows just how keen he is about the club.'

The tributes to Christie were a measure of his general popularity with the players. The fans too, as far as could be discerned from public comments, backed the manager. Gordon Graham, the treasurer of the Eastern Supporters Club, and a fan since Meadowbank were formed in 1974, said he could not believe that the man who had transformed the club from a 'joke team into a well-respected First Division outfit' could be treated like this. 'To force him to leave Meadowbank would be crass folly,' he insisted. Charlie Lawrie, who organised the Brake Club supporters, asked simply: 'Where are we going to get another manager with his experience, ability and commitment to Meadowbank Thistle?' Behind the scenes there was sympathy from other clubs too; Jack Steedman, then one of the owners of Clydebank, wrote a personal note to Christie saying how 'saddened' he was over the manager's recent problems – a copy was also sent to Blacklaw. In the letter Steedman added: 'It would be no consolation to you to hear that I often use your Club as an example of the maximum use of the minimum resources in Scottish football.' It was intended as a compliment to both Christie and Blacklaw for their stewardship of Meadowbank over the last dozen years. It was also to serve as an epitaph of the old regime at the club, where dramatic changes were not stopped by the end of season lull in the boardroom battle; merely delayed.

The Christie 'faction' may have won the propaganda skirmish over events at Meadowbank Thistle in recent weeks, but the public was not the only nor even the most important group to convince. The key constituency to win over in the Battle for Meadowbank were the 58 existing Founder Members who collectively still had the power to decide who ran the club and how. A meeting of the Founder Members was called for the end of the season, on 24th April; its task was to choose the members of a new management board of the club and effectively to decide the fate of the two rival groups. The end of the struggle was in sight.

Bill Hunter and Bill Mill were not going to allow the Founder Members to meet without them first hearing their own perspective on the club and recent events. The pair thus wrote a powerfully worded four-page letter to the members, justifying their own actions and putting forward their vision for the future. It did not hold back in its criticism. Some of this was aimed at John Blacklaw, for his unwillingness to 'act decisively' and sack Terry Christie. But mostly it was a strong and direct attack on Christie, his management style and his team's success – or lack of it – on the football field.

On the playing side Hunter and Mill said they disputed the suggestions – which had appeared in the media – that the manager had achieved success, especially in recent seasons. The club had won just six of its last 36 games, were currently third bottom (a position they maintained, at least saving relegation) as they had been the previous year, and had been saved from relegation only by other teams performing even more badly. The fact that Meadowbank had twice in recent season won the B&Q Fair Play Award 'unfortunately bears no relation to position in the League', the two men pointed out.

Another fault of Christie was that either by design or 'indifference to the Board' he apparently consulted or referred to no one else in the club when buying or selling players. Hunter and Mill informed the members that this included the recent sale of Christie's own son Max on 31 March, to Dundee, just nine months after buying him. The transfer fees had been identical – £30,000 – but the two men estimated that with taxes, insurances and fees the deal lost the club £14,000 (no mention was made of Bill Mill's exuberant public criticisms of Max Christie). This was just the tip of the iceberg; over the years Christie had brought in £340,000 in transfer fees from selling players but had spent some £500,000 in acquiring others, a loss to the club of more than £150,000. The manager had also allowed 5 players to go out of the contract at the same time, which would cost the club thousands in 'signing on' fees.

Some of the criticism was more personal. Christie had shown 'high handedness' in his dealings with the board and 'poor judgement' over financial matters and was overall a 'liability' to the entire club. They added: 'In its present state we feel there is no room at the Club for such egotism. The Club is more important than any one individual.'

The lengthy letter therefore made it clear that Hunter and Mill wanted Christie removed not just as manager but as a board member. The club's future was exciting, they said, but it needed to be re-structured and changed for the better; changes that Christie had 'opposed'. The letter's masterstroke, however, was to threaten the founder members where it really hurt – their pockets. In two devastating sentences it declared: 'we have long felt it is vital that a meeting of the members be held to consider a restructuring and refinancing of the Club.

'Otherwise we are faced with the possibility, should the club go into the "red", of each and every Founder Member being faced with paying the outstanding debt.'

The message was inescapable, and must have leapt out of the page to every single member, irrespective of what they thought of the rest of the letter; if you allow Christie to stay at the club, he will block any changes – and you could lose your shirt as a result.

The letter ended by pointing out that as John Blacklaw was retiring on 1 June, it would be a 'step in the right direction' if Bill Mill were to take his place.

The vehemence and urgency of the letter could not failed to have impressed the 58 Founder Members when it dropped through their letter boxes. It certainly had an impact on Terry Christie and Lawrie Glasson who then sent out their own 'reply' to the letter.

The Christie and Glasson letter first disputed the other's version of events surrounding the original vote of no confidence and the aftermath. It then took each of the main criticisms one by one, and responded to them. Christie had indeed always consulted John Blacklaw and got his approval for buying and selling players; the board had specifically delegated responsibility for this to the chairman. This had also been the case with the buying and selling of Max Christie (and this letter did refer to how Bill Mill would 'regularly and loudly scream abuse' at the youngster at away matches). There had been a small loss in the Christie deal – but less than half the amount claimed. As for the £500,000, Mill and Hunter claimed Christie had spent, there were no figures to back this up. In any case, the manager's sales had brought in £500,000 so even on the other side's figures the club had broken even. As for the 15 players out of contract – they were the reserve team who had been signed together and all put on two year contracts to give them a chance; an action acknowledged and approved at the time. And Christie insisted that as a director he had not opposed al change in the club structure; just that which allowed one person to take control. The five-page letter also dealt with the personalities of Bill Mill and Bill Hunter. Mill had served the club well and loyally for many years, it agreed, but pointed out that John Blacklaw – not Mill – had carried out many of the secretary's duties. Moreover, Mill's behaviour at away matches had been a 'constant source of embarrassment' to the club; the idea of this man being chairman of a Scottish league club made the mind 'boggle', said Glasson and Christie. As for Hunter; this self-styled 'football enthusiast' had watched only one reserve team game in ten months. He had also 'bombarded' the 'distinguished and honourable' John Blacklaw with legal letters, an indication, said the letter, of the lengths to which Hunter was prepared to go to achieve his ends.

In case anyone reading the letter had remaining doubts about what Christie and Glasson thought the fate of the club would be if they were ousted from the board, they made a final, impassioned plea. 'You should be clear that Bill Hunter seems set on obtaining a controlling interest in Meadowbank Thistle.

'If this is allowed to happen all stability will be lost from the Board Room down. Scottish football is notorious for the way in which small businessmen have grossly mis-managed football clubs.'

This letter attacking the Hunter and Mill position was every bit as strong and unforgiving as the one sent out by Mill and Hunter. If the founder members had entertained any doubts on the matter before, they were now left in now doubt there was no room for compromise between the two factions. Meadowbank Thistle simply wasn't big enough to contain the two main protagonists Bill Hunter and Terry Christie. One of them would have to go – and so it turned out.

When the votes were finally counted, it was clear that the Founder Members had produced a major victory for Bill Hunter. According to the count, each member of the club management committee (effectively the board of directors) was voted back onto the committee except one. That person was Terry Christie.

No one can be quite sure what swung the vote so decisively against Christie and in favour of Bill Mill and Bill Hunter. However, it is likely that the founder members had been concerned about the ramshackle structure of the club's set-up (one apparently said it was 'run along the lines of a bowling club') and were impressed with the need for the speedy change that Hunter promised. At the same time they had been warned (despite Christie's protestations to the contrary) that the manager/director opposed change, thus imperilling the members' own finances.

Terry Christie now realised that he had no choice but to resign as manager; had he stayed on he would surely have been fired. His assistant manager Tom Hendrie – a former striker at the club – also announced he would be resigning. The exodus was increased when Lawrie Glasson – who had been voted back on the board – also decided to resign from the club he had served so loyally, for so long. With John Blacklaw himself just a few weeks from his own retirement, this really did mark a major breach with the past. The Blacklaw/Christie partnership, which had been at the heart of the club since 1980, had come to an emphatic end.

Christie, the manager in the trademark duffel coat, has of course remained a familiar figure in Scottish football (and known to some fans still as 'The Duffle' because of his coat). He joined Stenhousemuir and more recently has been in charge at Alloa. All the time he remained part-time, insisting on putting his teaching career first until his retirement from the profession in 2003. That alone made his achievements at Meadowbank Thistle remarkable. During his twelve years at the club, Christie helped put the club on the footballing map in Scotland for all the right reasons. He took a poorly regarded Second Division team into the First Division, twice, and gave fans, players and officials alike good reason to be proud of Meadowbank Thistle. They say that all political careers end in failure; much the same can probably said of the careers of football managers. Even Terry Christie now admits that twelve years was perhaps too long to be in the same job, and that it was time to move on. He insists he feels not a scrap of bitterness towards Bill Hunter or anyone else. Indeed, Christie says the two men have spoken since those bitter spring days of 1992. At the time, it had been clear that the two men could not work together at the same club. Christie had had to go, though his pride was intact, and his legacy certain as the man who put first brought football success to Meadowbank.

As for Bill Hunter, he was left with a new company to set up, and with his ambitious plans for the club's future to fulfil. It would soon be clear that these plans would cause every bit as much drama and controversy as his boardroom battle with Terry Christie.

7

THE LURE OF LIVINGSTON

B
Y END OF THE SUMMER of 1992, Meadowbank Thistle had undergone fundamental change. The old axis of Terry Christie and John Blacklaw had gone (though the latter became Honorary President) as had director and former coach and assistant manager Lawrie Glasson and current assistant manager Tom Hendrie. The main link now with the past was the new chairman, Bill Mill, who had been with the club from its creation. For the new power at the club, Bill Hunter, however, the main focus of attention was not the club's past – but its future.

The April vote by the Founder Members – which had removed Christie from the board – had given Hunter and his ally Bill Mill an effective mandate to begin to change the club. The priority now was to sweep away the somewhat ramshackle administrative nature of the club (which was technically owned by the Founder Members) and replace it with a limited company that would be owned by the shareholders. In the meantime, the club desperately needed a new management board to help run the club after the mass exodus of the previous season. This new committee took up the reins after the start of the 1992/93 season. At the helm were the new chairman, Bill Mill, and the new secretary of the club Bill Hunter. They were joined by some new faces – and some interesting faces from the past. One of the new directors was John Bain, Meadowbank Thistle's first manager in 1974/75. Bain had later been obliged to sever his day-to-day links with the club when his work with Ferranti took him south to Derby for a number of years. Now he was back in Scotland and eager to help run the club with which he had been connected for 40 years. Another familiar face returning to Meadowbank was Hugh Cowan. Cowan was another who had played for Ferranti Thistle in the old days and then helped to run the club. He had been there at the formation of Meadowbank Thistle and had been its first vice-chairman until 1979 when work – Cowan was a mechanical design engineer at Ferranti – had also taken a position away from the area. Now he was back with his old title of vice-chairman. Thus, three veterans of the old Ferranti days – Mill, Bain, and Cowan – were reunited. Two new faces were Bob Clark and Walter Hay, the latter another former player at the club. Meanwhile the new team manager was

Donald Park, the former Hearts, Partick and Brechin midfielder, aided by assistant manager George Mackie.

Once the new team was in place, club secretary Hunter (whom most already recognised as the real driving force at the club) moved to change the constitution of the club. His solution to transfer the founder members into shareholders in a new limited company. At the same time, he would invest a significant amount of money – around £70,000 – into the club and would become the major shareholder. He now held 62,800 out of the 100,000 club shares. As secretary, director, and major shareholder, Bill Hunter, who on his own admission was a man who liked to lead from the front – would be in a strong position to determine the future direction of the club. The founder members, who were understandably anxious at the thought that they were currently liable for any debts the club might incur, were happy to vote through the change in structure to a limited company. By the summer of 1993, there was little doubt who was in control at Meadowbank Thistle: WP Hunter. The coup d'etat had taken place. In the months, ahead Hunter's abrupt seizure of power at the club was to be a major source of complaint from a section of the club's supporters. Just for now, though, fans and playing staff and something else on their minds – relegation.

One of the ostensible reasons Terry Christie had been removed as manager was because of the modest series of results on the pitch in recent seasons; fears of relegation from the First Division were never far away. Yet the team was to fare little better under Donald Park's stewardship. Park, who had played for Hearts, was later to become a much-respected coach at Edinburgh rivals Hibernian. But even he could not quickly change Meadowbank Thistle's fortunes. The side was quickly dumped out of the League Cup at home by Dundee, then equally swiftly dispatched from the Scottish Cup away at Dundee United. In the league, the top scorer was new striker Paul Rutherford with a modest tally of nine goals, and once more Meadowbank struggled to score enough goals and pick up wins.

There were some brighter, quirkier moments, as for example when for the first time in its club history Meadowbank fielded a first team player who was younger than the club itself. Martin O'Connell had been born in September 1974 – a month after Thistle were re-formed from Ferranti – and now eighteen-year-old O'Connell was making his debut for the club. Another youngster who was already forging a name for himself was Ian Little. Blooded in the first team at just 16, he was now 19 and had already chalked up 100 appearance, as well as being caped by Scotland at under-18 level.

Yet with home gates still averaging under 600 a game, the 1992/93 season was in every other way looking as bad on the field as the previous one; then as Thistle dropped ominously into eleventh place (out of twelve) it got even worse. After six successive seasons in the First Division, and in the new regime of Bill Hunter and Bill Mill, Meadowbank were relegated back to the Second Division. Though not perhaps a shock for the fans, relegation still came as a bitter blow. The swift demise of long-serving manager Christie and the abrupt rise to prominence of Bill Hunter had already caused disquiet among some of the regulars who turned up at Meadowbank Stadium and away games. The unease may have reduced had the new regime swiftly delivered success on the field. Now, though, Thistle were back in the Second Division and back where they had started. The rumbles of discontent with the club set-up would soon grow massively in scale until it turned into full-scale war between the club hierarchy and a core of supporters. But the poor results would not be the only, nor even the main reason for this new battle of Meadowbank. The issue that would dominant the club for the next two years was even more fundamental than just results. The battle would be over the very identity and location of the club.

Though the Commonwealth Stadium had been Meadowbank's home since its creation, the ground had always been a hard one to live with. Apart from anything else, it was just so different from other football grounds and certainly lacked their sense of the dramatic (a common observation was that it had 'less atmosphere than the moon'). This was no fault of the stadium; it had after all been built primarily to house athletics events, which have very different demands from football matches. In the mid-1980's there had been some improvements at the ground, notably new changing rooms. This upgrade had helped to take away some of the criticism from visiting teams about cramped facilities at the venue. But the vast emptiness of the arena, the remoteness of the main stand and the sterility of the atmosphere were near impossible to change. In addition, there was the problem caused by too many events (especially in the spring and late summer) competing for the same dates at the ground. The owners, the district council, had to juggle the bookings to try and keep everyone happy; much to the dismay of both Meadowbank Thistle and the Scottish football authorities. John Bain recalled his early days as manager. 'If [the council] wanted a function on under the main stand they could put it on at a minute's notice and scupper our football. 'Sometimes I'd get a call a week before a game saying "You can't play next weekend because we're having a cat show and Mrs So-and-so doesn't want her animals disturbed by rowdy football fans".

'Dog shows, flower shows, you name it. There were all sorts of reasons for games being cancelled and it was really starting to upset the Scottish League.'

In fact the council did do their best to help, but they were in an impossible situation.

However the fact that the ground was not well-suited to football and had to compete with other events for time and space were not the club's main concern. Nor was it the fact that they rented rather than owned the ground; for 18 years John Blacklaw had run the club in the black without needing the help of any capital assets.

The real problem with the club – certainly as seen by Bill Hunter and others connected with the club – was its very location in Edinburgh. Ever since its formation, Meadowbank Thistle had sat firmly in the shadow of the capital's 'Big Two', Hearts and Hibs. Even after gaining promotion to the First Division and so narrowly missing elevation to the Premier Division, the club's junior third club status had barely changed. This was particularly noticeable in Thistle's core fan base. Its biggest crowd at the ground – more than 4,000 against Stirling Albion – had come in Meadowbank's very first competitive game. Since then the average attendances had been, to say the least, quite disappointing. For some home games the club was lucky to see two or three hundred people tramp through the gates. The highest average for a season was in 1988/89, the year after they early made the top rung of Scottish football, when around 850 people regularly turned up for home fixtures. The more usual average, however, was between five and six hundred.

Realistically, the only way to improve the Meadowbank Stadium attendances was by the club reaching and staying in the Premier Division and attracting fans who would regularly come to watch clubs such as Celtic, Rangers, Aberdeen, plus Hearts and Hibs. To do this, however, the club would require a large injection of money and a larger revenue stream to pay the transfer fees and wages of the players they would need to stay in the Premier Division. This kind of money was only likely to come from one source – more paying customers. And it was the lack of these that was causing the problems in the first place. As Terry Christie has since noted, Meadowbank Thistle was the best-performing part-time club in Scottish football at the time, but it was punching above its weight. Even to remain in the First Division had been a struggle, and had been beyond the club in 1992/93 when they dropped down. Nor was life back in the Second Division likely to help in increasing the club's core fan base. The blunt fact was that Edinburgh did not seem able to support three 'big' teams. There was certainly no doubting the loyalty and depth of Meadowbank's existing supporters. The problem was that there were just too few of them; and if nothing was done to bring about major changes, then the club would gradually drift towards oblivion.

This was how the argument of Hunter and like-minded officials ran in the early 1990's. The counter-argument was of course that all this only mattered if you wanted or expected Meadowbank Thistle to be one of the big clubs who were in or around the Premier Division permanently. Those hardy fans who did turn up week, week out to watch Thistle play, had been largely content with the performance of the team in recent years. As their remarks at the time of the Christie crisis showed, they were grateful to him for having lifted the club's football status from 'joke' team to a respectable First (or Second) Division side. The supporters by and large enjoyed themselves and had a good rapport with the players and coaching staff. The 'Wee Bankies' fans had a deserved reputation for intense loyalty and a fine sense of humour. It was true that in current circumstances the side was never likely to challenge for European honours, but it was no embarrassment either; and the club was not in debt. Put like this, was there any real need to consider widespread changes? Why could the club not continue along the same lines, albeit with different (and in fans' eyes better) management, as they had under the Blacklaw regime?

The answer to these questions really depends on your philosophy regarding supporting a football team. It might be that you are content to watch a middling team display middling performances, and simply enjoy the experience of familiarity and unique bond with your team. Yes, success would be great – but was not worth huge sacrifices. On the other hand, you might be ambitious for change and success from your side, and willing to consider (almost) anything to achieve it. Both are honourable and respectable points of view. Broadly speaking, the core Meadowbank fans fell into the former category, and Bill Hunter into the latter.

It would be wrong to see Hunter as the only person who was deeply ambitious for success and change. It should be remembered who the men now around him were and what they had done. John Bain had helped take Ferranti Thistle from the city welfare leagues into the East of Scotland

League; Bain, Bill Mill and Hugh Cowan had taken Ferranti into full membership of the Scottish Football Association and then overseen its transition to Meadowbank Thistle and gaining membership of the Scottish League. These were driven men, and age had not dimmed all their ambitions. They were keen for success and were not keen to see the club settling in the Second Division or lower reaches of the First Division, and with perennially low attendances. The question for them was how to achieve this success. The answer, or so they believed, came from Bill Hunter.

Bill Hunter had decided that if the club wanted to progress, indeed if it wanted to survive at all, it simply had to move. The only question left to answer – though it was a big one – was where.

There had been plans earlier in Meadowbank's history to relocate from the Commonwealth Stadium. The most advanced of these was the project to redevelop the site of the old open-air swimming baths at Portobello. Opened in 1936, the 330-feet long pool, complete with wave-making machine, had once been an immensely popular attraction both before and after the Second World War. However, it gradually lost its appeal and fell into disuse; by 1980 it was closed. A number of local businessmen had joined forces with Meadowbank in the mid-1980's to suggest that the site could be a new home for the club, together with a larger leisure complex. In the end the idea had foundered after local opposition and uncertainty over whether enough capital could be raised. (The site has now been turned into a smart leisure complex by Edinburgh City Council.) In any case, moving to Portobello would hardly have addressed the central reason for re-locating Meadowbank, which was to attract a whole new fan base to the club. It seems Bill Hunter's original plan had been to move the club eastwards of Edinburgh to east Lothian. Hunter himself was from Prestopans in East Lothian and knew the area well and had many local contacts. East Lothian, which has a population of around 85,000 people, was already well-known for two sports; horse-racing at Musselburgh and of course golf at one of the world's great courses, Muirfield. Perhaps league football could become another sporting attraction and tap into the latent support in the area. The dream was to develop the existing ground at Olive Bank in Musselburgh, already home to junior side Musselburgh Athletic. This, like the earlier Portobello plans, failed to materialise after Bill Hunter could not find a solution to structure the deal which was suitable to all parties.

In the meantime, however, another intriguing possibility had raised itself. Instead of moving east, which were Hunter's natural inclinations, why not move the football club west – to West Lothian? The idea of moving west apparently came by chance at a race meeting in 1992, when Bill Hunter was discussing the club's projected move to East Lothian. One of those present was an official of the Livingston Development Corporation, who suggested that rather than heading east, Meadowbank should consider moving west instead. Specifically, the club should come to the new town of Livingston. And so, from this chance encounter, the idea of Meadowbank Thistle relocating to Livingston emerged. There were of course immediate objections; neither the club nor its personnel had any connection with Livingston, it was some way outside Edinburgh, and existing Thistle fans would have to travel almost as far for 'home' matches as they would for some away games.

Yet now that the idea of moving to Livingston had been mentioned, it slowly began to make some sense to Bill Hunter and others at the club. By the early 1990's the new town had a population of around 45,000 and even more importantly it was quite a young population – the average age was just 29. Just over a quarter of the town's population was under the age of sixteen. Yet, there was nowhere locally for this youthful population to channel their passion for football. True, there was a junior side called Livingston, but there was no league club nearby. This led to many football fans travelling to Edinburgh, Glasgow or further afield at weekends to watch top League matches. Here surely was the captive football audience that Bill Hunter and the board of directors at Meadowbank Thistle had been searching. It was inconceivable that a town of this size – combined with the surrounding catchment area such as Bathgate – could not attract more than the few hundred fans per home game that Meadowbank currently received. Though Livingston would provide a journey for existing Meadowbank fans, the town was at least well-placed for transport connections with both Edinburgh – 18 miles away – and Glasgow, which is 30 miles to the west.

Livingston was also a town that saw itself with a strong future. Historically, West Lothian had relied on the coal industry to provide jobs. When this industry disappeared, the area went into decline and by the early 1960's, there was little work to be found locally. Livingston was developed as a new town (the fourth of Scotland's five post-war new towns) to house workers from Glasgow to the west, and in doing so had attracted some industry of its own, notably a British Leyland car plant. Yet by the early 1980's the area was once more suffering economically and a

'West Lothian economic summit' in 1981 hammered out plans to bring new industry to the area, including Livingston. At the forefront of this attempt to breath life into the area was the Livingston Development Corporation (LDC), which had been established in the 1960's to develop the new town. At its peak, the LDC employed around 1,000 people in the town. Its task was to plan and oversee the development of new houses, new factories and industrial plants, civic buildings, the layout of roads and public amenities such as leisure centres. The LDC and other local bodies had, during the late 1980's , been largely successful in making Livingston a thriving town and a popular. The evidence of this was in the youthful and rapidly rising population. So if Meadowbank were to move from Edinburgh, Livingston was beginning to look like the best option. However, there as another factor to be taken into consideration – would Livingston want Meadowbank Thistle?

Despite its growing self-confidence and increased amenities, Livingston still felt like a new town. Economically it was now successful; socially it was less so. Naturally enough there were few traditions or shared experiences to unite the population. One of the factors that can unite a town, bind its people together and forge its identity is the presence of a thriving sports team. This was something Livingston lacked, certainly in proportion to its growing size. The result was that a certain something was lacking from Livingston. To quote Tony Kinder, now a director of Livingston FC, and a local councillor in the area: 'It was.... recognised that Livingston was without soul.' Or as some promotional literature from the LDC was later to put it in marketing-speak: 'LDC sees the provision of a senior football club within Livingston as the final chain of events that will unite the community.'

The LDC, and in particular its chief executive Jim Pollock, realised the potential of the football club moving there; and as usual the corporation was not slow in pushing its case with vigour.

In other words, the idea of re-locating Meadowbank Thistle from the capital to the new town of Livingston was seen as a win-win situation for both sides (apart from the Thistle fans who simply saw it as a lose-lose). The football club would win living space, a total catchment population of up to 150,000 and a chance to forge a new and bigger identity in a new area. For the new town itself, the arrival of a football league football team would be the final bit of social glue to bind the town's community together. Top-flight football would give the community a heart and focus, not to mention some very good new sporting facilities. The problem was, for both parties, that the relocation would cost money. The biggest cost by far, would be a new stadium in Livingston; nothing as yet existed that could cope with a football league team in the town.

Once Bill Hunter and members of the LDC had decided – by late 1992 – that the project was both desirable and possible, detailed negotiations began to take place.

Initially these talks were to be in secret; after all there was no point in raising hopes (in Livingston) or fears (among Meadowbank fans) if the plans were to founder on the reefs of commercial reality. On the Meadowbank side, the main negotiator was Bill Hunter himself, though other directors were involved in the deliberations. For the LDC the lead players was Jim Pollock and commercial director David Balfour. The man who would take the lead role in finding the right location and designing both the ground and the other facilities that would accompany it was LDC senior surveyor Tom Dickie.

Thought also had to be given to the future; by 1997 the LDC was to be wound down as Livingston lost its new town status. The possibility of bringing league football to the area would be one of the last, and certainly one of the biggest, of the corporation's achievements in the town. This meant that the West Lothian district council, who would take on many of the administrative functions locally, had to be brought on board to ensure that the project would be supported in the future.

The intention was to build a purpose-built stadium in the heart of Livingston, with seats for 4,000 people and with enough capacity to extend this if necessary to 10,000. This last proviso was both a sensible future-proof piece of planning as well as a sign of the club's ambitions. After all, in the light of the Taylor Report into football stadia (which followed the 1989 Hillsborough Disaster) the minimum requirement for entering the Premier Division from now on would be enough seats for 10,000 fans. Hunter and his club were certainly planning ahead.

The new ground would be in the Almondvale district of the town, not far from the Almondvale shopping centre and bordered on one side by the River Almond and another by Almondvale Park. It would have parking for more than 400 cars, and good road and rail access to Edinburgh and Glasgow. The LDC were intending to promote the project under their current and final slogan 'Make it in Livingston'. As yet the proposed new stadium did not have a name. Even more importantly, neither did the club – if and when it moved. If Meadowbank Thistle were to make this dramatic leap and uproot from Edinburgh to Livingston, then the name of the new club would be key. It was clear from the start that the name Meadowbank Thistle itself would not remain; there would be little point in moving to a new town with the aim of attracting new fans and then not identifying the club's name with the new location. For the LDC it was inconceivable not to insist on having Livingston in the name of the 'new' club – this was central to their aim of bringing identity and 'soul' to the community after all. Yet at this early stage no decisions had been reached on the precise name. Intriguingly, some early LDC literature referred to the 'Livingston Meadow FC Concept' and the 'Livingston Meadow FC Partnership'. The most obvious name discussed at this time was a straight amalgam of the club and the new location – Livingston Thistle. This would have the advantage of giving the club a clear sense of geography while at the same time preserving part of the club's heritage back through Meadowbank Thistle to Ferranti Thistle. Inevitably this crucial issue of the name of the club would play a central role in the bitter controversy that would break out over Meadowbank's plans to move from the capital; at the heart of this row would be the reaction of the club's fans.

The news of Meadowbank's interest in moving to Livingston inevitably became public. Bill Hunter had already made it clear that he believed the club needed to adapt or die – and the adaptation meant changing its environment. The LDC and the club also needed to carry out some market research to be sure that a league club would – as everyone suspected – be welcomed by the West Lothian populace. It would have been impossible to justify large amounts of public money being spent on the project – and the LDC would have to be the biggest fund provider – without all the parties being able to demonstrate popular support for the idea. It was not a concept that one could keep secret for long.

The Meadowbank fans had already been wary of Bill Hunter. Most of them had been fans of Terry Christie and what he had done for the team over the years. Many of them also had respected the gentlemanly chairmanship of John Blacklaw. Both these two men had gone and the whole structure of the club was changing. Bill Hunter was now indisputably the man in charge and seemed to be determined to take the club in new directions; but would they be directions the fans wanted to go? The answer was not long in coming. Over the summer of 1993 the news of discussions between Meadowbank Thistle and Livingston Development Corporation became public. A hard core of fans made it clear that they objected to the moves on two very obvious points – the move would mean leaving Edinburgh and it would entail changing the club's name. Neither of these were acceptable to this relatively small but vociferous group of fans. 'This will mean the death of the club,' quickly became a common refrain among these supporters. One of the early clashes came between the club and David Baxter, a long-standing and loyal Thistle fan. He had previously edited the club's official programme but after his views on the club's move became known, Baxter was removed from this voluntary position. Now the editor of *The Thistle*, the fans' fanzine, Baxter had been involved in an incident at a home match at the start of the 1993/94 season, when he had been removed from the ground by stewards. Baxter later explained that he had originally entered the ground using a complimentary ticket, but had subsequently re-entered as a paying customer.

In the media, the start of a war of words began between a section of the supporters and Bill Hunter and other club officials.

Supporter Colin McPherson, said that fans were deeply sceptical of the claims been made of the supposed benefits of the move. He told *The Herald*: 'The market research on this has been ridiculously flimsy, amounting to standing outside a shopping centre in Livingston and questioning passers-by.

'I'm not convinced about the economic arguments for moving out there. [Mr Hunter] is talking about 1500 bums on seats at every home game to break even. Look around the league — not many clubs are getting that.'

Bill Hunter however, claimed a majority of the fans were in favour of the move. He added: 'We are optimistic that we will be playing at Livingston next year.'

At this stage, however, the deal was far from certain and Hunter's words were rather optimistic. In the early autumn of 1993 the LDC were still undertaking 'feasibility studies' to see if the plan really had a commercial as well as a social justification. The two parties had exchanges letters of intent, stating that the two sides were in principle agreed on the move. But this was still very much at an outline stage. The cost was becoming clearer – around £6million – and the terms under which the football club would use the club – in a 125-year lease. Yet the crucial details of the financial structuring of the deal were still to be decided. The principle funders of the development would inevitably be the Livingston Development Corporation, but it was also hoped that other backers would come on board as well; chiefly the Football Trust (who were in turn funded by Littlewoods Pools), the Sports Council and the Scottish Football Association. Negotiations between so many partners were bound to take their time.

As the talks progressed in 1993, the mutual antagonism between the club hierarchy – and in particular Bill Hunter – and a section of fans increased in frequency and intensity. A considerable amount of abuse was thrown at the club's major shareholder. On one occasion, Hunter was so angry at one fan's abuse that he chased after him to remonstrate with him; the businessman later explained that he had felt especially aggrieved on this occasion as the perpetrator had used foul language in the presence of his teenage daughter. Whatever the justification for the event, it only served to fuel the bitterness of the two sides.

With the internecine war bloodier than ever, this was perhaps not the ideal time to show the future folk of Livingston what they could expect from the second division side. Yet the board was determined to keep up the momentum of the plans. So it was that a group of slightly bemused families from the new town were invited to Meadowbank Thistle's home Scottish Cup tie with Montrose on January 8, 1994. This trip, which cost £6 for a group of three including transport, also took in a trip round the Meadowbank Stadium and a visit to the dressing rooms. To what extent the visitors to Edinburgh were impressed is hard to say. Thistle lost the second round tie 2-1 in a game that was no great advert for football. At least the meagre crowd of 339 would have impressed one important fact upon the new town visitors – that the club's fan base badly needed to be increased. It was also a reminder to everyone what the club was supposed to be about – playing football matches. The entire 1993/94 was overshadowed by events off the field. Yet despite all these unwanted and unfortunate distractions, the team was performing reasonably well. The youthful Ian Little appeared in every league match, and was the club's top scorer with twelve league goals. The side's cup performance was, admittedly, disappointing again. The defeat against Montrose had followed an early exit from the League Cup at the hands of Dundee – though only after penalties. Yet after finding its feet once more in the Second Division the team stayed in the top half of the division, ultimately finishing fourth out of 14. This was even more laudable considering that the players not only had to put up with the off-stage noises from the Hunter/fan row, but with a double change of manager too. After the temporary reign of Donald Park, John Brownlie took over in charge of the side at the end of 1993, with Gordon Brown as his assistant. The former Hibs and Scotland full back, who had previously been assistant manager at Clyde, did not stay long at the helm of the club however. After just six weeks and seven games as manager, Brownlie quit because of his work. A recent promotion had made it necessary for him to work on some weekends, creating a conflict with his footballing responsibilities. The new boss was to be Mickey Lawson, a familiar face at the club that he had served well both as a player and off the pitch too over the years. The much-travelled Lawson had also been at Musselburgh Athletic, Stirling Albion, St Johnstone, Raith Rovers, and Berwick Rangers. But Lawson had been a loyal servant at Meadowbank, and had also been a popular figure with the fans. Indeed, it was his goal on 7 May 1983 away at Brechin that had secured the draw that saw Thistle promoted for the first time to the First Division for the first time. Yet if the appointment of Mickey Lawson and the strong showing in the league were consolations, they were, set against the bigger back drop of the impending move, scant ones for the fans.

It was true that the timetable for the club's move was looking in jeopardy; by the late winter of 1994, the final deal with the LDC was far from signed, despite the determination of both sides to make it work. Bill Hunter, however, gave no sign of having any doubts about the wisdom of the relocation, and certainly no intention of bowing to the wishes of the Thistle fans who opposed it.

'Meadowbank cannot survive the way it is going at present,' he bluntly told journalists who questioned him over the on-going row with the fans. 'We have a hard core of around 100 supporters, and even a few seasons ago when we were near the top of the First Division it wasn't much more.' The businessman also insisted that the number of fans vehemently opposed to the move numbered only about 30. 'They're supposed to be supporters but they have done nothing but orchestrate a vendetta against the club,' he argued.

For their part the fans, including former programme editor Dave Baxter, were adamant that the battle – or war as some described it – was about the very existence of Meadowbank Thistle. 'You are witnessing the death of a football club,' Baxter told the media at the time. The fans also objected to the fact that Hunter had taken control of the club, and that they, the fans who had helped keep to club going for years, seemed to have no say in its future direction. As Baxter pointed out: 'Supporters have never been given a chance to say to Hunter "No, we don't want you".'

The language from both sides proved that there was little room for compromise; not did there seem to be much appetite for it either. As winter gave way to spring, the 'War of Meadowbank' got bloodier and more personal. For the second time in a short period Meadowbank Thistle – a name once synonymous with a harmonious, quietly-run club – was making newspaper headlines of entirely the wrong kind.

Bill Hunter had been growing increasingly impatient of the abuse that was being thrown his way; in particular his rotund figure had earned him the unkind nickname of 'Mr Blobby' among a sector of the supporters. The disturbances grew. On 12 March, at home to division leaders Stranraer, Thistle managed a good 1-1 draw. But all the headlines were dominated by the protests of some of the spectators. Though all the directors were criticised for the planned move, it was Bill Hunter once again who was singled out for the most attention. 'Mr Blobby, Out! Out! Out!' called a section of the crowd of 453. Then just before half time police officers had to intervene to calm matters down when exchanges between fans and club stewards threatened to get out of hand. The fans had objected to attempts by the stewards to eject one of their number; after the police stepped in the atmosphere was calmer. However, though no arrests were made, this was the beginning of a grim period in Meadowbank Thistle's history. Irrespective of one's views about the wisdom or otherwise of the relocation, it was sad to see the club's reputation being dragged through the mud so publicly.

The next home game, against Stenhousemuir on 19 March, saw the conflict plummet to new depths. On a day described in some media reports as 'The Afternoon of the Long Knives' four Meadowbank fans were removed and banned from the ground. One of them was ejected for shouting: 'This is a dictatorship!'; another for loudly informing Bill Hunter 'You're living in dreamland, Blobby!'. The ugly scenes were even more striking for taking place in a crowd of just 218 spectators. They also overshadowed a 1-0 win by Thistle, and the return to the ground of Stenhousemuir player Graeme Armstrong, who was making his 700th league appearance, and at the ground where he had played many of them – as a popular Meadowbank players for many years.

The fans had now set up a body to fight the club's proposed move and what they saw as Bill Hunter's autocratic behaviour. Known as the Thistle Action Group, it collected a petition in Edinburgh against the plans to move the club and change its name. Some of the fans likened the plans to a 'kidnapping' of the club by Bill Hunter. This explains why when the petition was handed over by Meadowbank fan Gordon Buchanan to local PM Dr Gavin Strang, the supporter was dressed as David Balfour – the hero of Robert Louis Stevenson's famous novel *Kidnapped*.

The petition had the impressive figure of 4,238 signatures supporting it, and like any good constituency, MP Dr Strang took it seriously and promised to deliver it to the club's directors. Referring to the club's history in Edinburgh, the MP Dr Strang said: 'Ferranti Thistle and Meadowbank Thistle are an important element of Edinburgh's football heritage. It's important that the move being proposed will enhance the club in the long-term.'

However, critics pointed out that many of the signatures had been collected at the city's railway stations and may well have been signed by fans of other clubs, including some from Glasgow, which would have undermined its impact. Thistle's new club secretary Jim Renton – a former top flight referee in Scotland – was also less than impressed by the petition. 'They should have collected names from the 200 who watch Meadowbank on Saturday,' he said.

Nothing, moreover, seemed likely to deter Bill Hunter from pursuing his dream of moving the club. The next big hurdle for the club's board to overcome was to get official Scottish Football Association approval for the decision to relocate the SFA member club and re-name it.

The SFA insisted publicly that they were keeping an open mind on the subject, and that there was no question of rubber-stamping the move. In particular there had been speculation that the SFA might insist on the name Livingston Thistle. This would serve the double purpose of preserving part of the club's heritage while also making it clear that the new league club in the new town were not related to junior sides such as Livingston United. A number of media commentators had identified the name of Livingston Thistle as a happy compromise between the traditionalists and those who wanted to effect major change at the club.

SFA official Jim Farry told *Scotland on Sunday*: 'I've received many a tear-stained letter on the subject, and we'll be fair in our deliberations. I certainly wouldn't say it's a foregone conclusion it will go through.'

However, when the SFA announced their ruling on 25 April, few observers were surprised at their verdict: Meadowbank were given permission to change their name to Livingston FC.

For the fans who opposed the move and the new name, it was a crippling, and effectively a final blow. Their defeat was not for want of trying; some fans had even tried to set up a consortium in a vain attempt to buy control of the club. As David Baxter of the Thistle Action Group, and who himself was ejected from the ground without explanation, said at the time: 'We might be small fry, but we're going to fight this. [Hunter is] killing off Meadowbank. He's changing our name, changing our venue, making a new club that doesn't resemble the Thistle we support.'

Yet the SFA ruling effectively meant Hunter had won, and that despite the continued protests nothing could now stop the move and the new name.

Of all the issues involved, it was the failure of the club to compromise even a little and adopt the name 'Thistle' that hurt the most. This had, after all, been the name the club had used since the days of Ferranti Thistle from the early 1950's and had been retained in the current name of Meadowbank Thistle. It was clear to just about everyone that if the club needed to move to Livingston to survive, then the club had to adopt the name of its new home. (It will also be recalled that Meadowbank had never wanted to be called 'Meadowbank' in the first place; the Scottish League had demanded the club change its name from Ferranti and the council owners of the club's new rented ground insisted they adopt the name of the stadium.) But was it really necessary to lose the epithet 'Thistle' as well? The failure to retain this part of the name caused anguish at the time even among those who supported the club's relocation; and it still rankles with some today who embrace the tremendous success of Livingston FC. If The Scottish League had been guilty of an act of cultural vandalism in forcing Ferranti to change its name to Meadowbank, then here was an act of self-mutilation by the club. Livingston Thistle would indeed have been the perfect compromise.

However, Livingston FC it was to be; the name was thought to be simpler, bolder and easier to market as being of the new town if there were no qualifications attached to it.

If the fans were now fighting a fruitless cause, there were still frustrations at Meadowbank about the likely speed of the project. It had been hoped that work could begin on the still unnamed stadium at Almondvale by August 1994. Yet as the 1993/94 season came to an end, and the brief summer recess also finished, there was still no sight of a signed deal. Part of the delay was in finalising funding details; another was in deciding who should get to build the new stadium. Despite constant assurances to the media that work on the new stadium would begin soon, the starting date for work on the project slowly crept backwards. Eventually a site opening ceremony was announced for December 12th, around two years after discussions had begun between Meadowbank and the LDC. The main contractors for the stadium were to be Mowlem Scotland Limited. The main funding was to come from the LDC, but the Football Trust had also pledged a generous £500,000 towards the scheme. Meanwhile the Scottish Football association were helping fund the closed circuit television network at the stadium, the Sports Council were helping pay for the electrical services while Lothian and Edinburgh Enterprise were helping to shape the area around the stadium. The project – now estimated to cost £5million – had as its centrepiece a two-stand floodlit football pitch. But it was also to include for four five-a-side football pitches, a synthetic football pitch, a conference centre, restaurant, Members social club and, a sign of the times a crèche.

There were no signs at the news conference announcing the start of this ambitious project of the bitter controversy that it had created back at Meadowbank's existing home. The local great and the good lined up to heap praise on the development. LDC chairman Bob Watt heralded it as an 'historic event' for the town; Peter Johnston, chairman of West Lothian District Council's Environmental Health and Leisure Services Committee insisted the arrival of league football would provide a major boost for the area. 'Football is close to the heart of everyone in West Lothian and I am delighted that at long last the County has an opportunity to support a local football team.'

The remarks by Bill Hunter would have been hardest to bear for many of the core Meadowbank fans. Describing himself as 'euphoric' over the move he added: 'We are looking forward to the new start in front of a mix of old and new fans. We have suffered in the past from being the third club in Edinburgh – but now we have the opportunity to create a real identity for ourselves in one of the most football-minded communities in the whole of Scotland.'

Those fans might have queried, had they been present, just what had been wrong with the old 'identity' of Meadowbank Thistle. However, many others connected with the club felt that something special was about to happen. Here was the chance to create what the original post-war founders of the club had dreamt of many years ago; a football team with a real chance of competing with the best. Some even agreed with the words of Tom 'Tiny' Wharton, the deputy chairman of the Football Trust when he said: 'I have no doubt this venture will be a success. Bill Hunter is a man of vision and courage.'

For Hunter himself, it was the culmination of many months of work, during which the pressures had been intense. He had undergone a major heart operation and seen himself, wife, and daughter the subjects of taunts and abuse – including abusive calls to his house. He revealed to journalists that he had even though of quitting the club because of what he and his family were suffering, but ill Hunter was not a man to give up without a fight. 'I decided [they] were not going to beat me,' he said, referring to some of his most bitter critics. As the mechanical diggers began their work at Almondvale, it was clear that Hunter had won his battle.

The days of Meadowbank Thistle were not quite over, however. The delays in starting the new stadium at Almondvale meant that the relocation would not be in time for any part of the 1994/95 season – in fact, it would not be ready for the start of the following season either. This meant that the 1994/95 campaign had to be fought out under the old name of Meadowbank at their old rented ground at the Meadowbank Stadium. In many ways, it was the season no one wanted. For the club hierarchy, impatient to move, it was a year of treading water until they could get to the 'future' at Livingston. Meanwhile Thistle fans had to endure the prospect of watching for an entire season a team they already knew was disappearing – at least in its existing form – next year. Inevitably this was reflected both in results on the pitch – as well as in attendances. This season saw an average of just 295 fans turn up for home matches, the second lowest in the club's league history (the lowest was back in 1981/82). Those that did turn up were still fiercely loyal to their team; but they felt it would not be their team much longer. And it is hard to muster too much enthusiasm for a team whom you know will not be there next season; part of the joy of being a fan is the hope (or dream) that things will be better next year. For those fans who saw little or no continuity between Meadowbank Thistle and Livingston, there was no 'next year'.

The club had also clashed again with the fans, this time by refusing to recognise the official supporters club unless and until it complied with certain conditions such as supplying a complete list of members, together with their addresses. For the fans, it was tantamount to a vetting process.

A spokesman for the supporters John McKirdy gave the reaction of the fans to this latest clash with Thistle officialdom. 'This is an outrage. The supporters club is a democratic organisation. The membership is the best judge of who is fit or unfit to run it — not Mr Hunter or any other director.'

To no one's surprise, it was clear there were going to be no last minute reconciliation between Bill Hunter and the fans who opposed the club's massive changes. Nor was there going to be a fairy tale ending to the club's last season on the field of play, either. Under a reorganisation of the league, there were now four divisions of ten teams, with a Third Division in place below the Second. This meant that finishing at the bottom of the Second Division was no longer simply embarrassing – it signalled relegation too. A chronic inability to score was the main reason for Thistles' problems that season. The top league scorer was Lee Bailey, who managed six goals. They had little luck in the League Cup either; after beating Stenhousemuir 4-0 in the first round, they went down 4-1 at Dunfermline. The performance in the Scottish Cup was a little more promising, as victories over Forfar and Berwick set up an exciting away tie at Parkhead in front of more than 23,000 fans; in the circumstances a 3-0 defeat was almost respectable. Yet it was the league that really mattered, and where Thistle stumbled badly. By the time a disconsolate Mickey Lawson resigned in March 1995 – ending his hopes of taking them to Livingston – the club were already in trouble at the foot of the Second Division. The arrival of a new manager – Jim Leishman lifted morale. But though Leishman was to have a major role in the club's future fortunes, even he could not save them from the drop. In their last season as Meadowbank Thistle, the club finished ninth out of ten – and were relegated to the Third Division. If the move to Livingston was to be a new dawn for the club, then the darkest moment had taken place just before it. There was a certain irony too about one of the clubs that Meadowbank would now meet in the bottom rung of Scottish league football; Inverness Caledonian Thistle. Inverness had recently been admitted to the league (along with Ross County) to make number of clubs up to 40, allowing four equally sized divisions. The Highland club was the new amalgam of two well-known clubs of the past, Inverness Caledonian and Inverness Thistle. The latter was the club whom Meadowbank (as Ferranti) had surprisingly and controversially beaten in the vote to become a league member back in 1974.

Mourned by a few hundred dedicated fans, the 21-year history of Meadowbank Thistle had come to an inglorious and unsatisfactory end. For those supporters, the Meadowbank club had died at the end of that season and its obituaries could be written. Yet among other, and new fans, the club was simply entering a new phase. The name and the ground may have changed; but the spirit of the old Ferranti days would live on with a fresh start and in a new town – Livingston.

8

The Lion's Roar

THE START OF THE 1995/96 was certainly an odd one; new town, new name – but the same old ground. The delays in starting the construction of the new stadium at Almondvale had meant that the club's proposed new home at Livingston would not be ready in time for the start of the next season. Therefore for the first few games at least, the new team – Livingston – would have to play back at their former home of 20 years, the old Commonwealth Stadium. It was an inauspicious start for Bill Hunter and everyone else at the new club. Nor was it the ideal way for Livingston to start to build up a fresh fan base – the main reason behind the relocation and name change in the first place. For some weeks, therefore, the familiar concrete surroundings of the old Meadowbank ground would serve as a reminder both of the club's short but proud history there, and the bitterness over its decision to leave.

Yet the club was nevertheless very optimistic and fiercely ambitious. The directors were determined to make Livingston a fully professional club as soon as possible, knowing that otherwise their main aim – Premier League football for the new town – would be impossible.

To mark the start of a new era the club sported new shirts. They had kept the clubs traditional colours – black and amber – but the main emphasis in the new strips was on black. It was a distinctive look, and the black-shirted team did indeed cut an impressive sight when the side played its first match under the Livingston name. This was against Montrose at Links Park in the first round of the League (Coca Cola) Cup. It was hard to detect many Livingston fans in the away crowd; perhaps this was hardly surprising given that the club was not really based anywhere at present and was stuck in something of a football twilight zone. But the team – many of whom were familiar faces from the Meadowbank days – were determined to rise to this small moment of history. Livingston's first, historic goal was scored by Jason Young, and when Grant McMartin knocked in the second it was enough to earn the peripatetic club a 2-0 win in their opening game.

The second round then provided one of the early high spots in the new Third Division's side's existence. Though the attendance at league games was to prove disappointing in the early homeless weeks of the season, a sizeable contingent of new Livingston fans did make their way to

McDiarmid Park to see their side take on First Division St Johnstone in the cup. They were not disappointed. Lee Bailey, the previous year's top scorer, put the Third Division side ahead, only for the Perth team's George O'Boyle to level the score. After a goalless extra time the tie went to penalties, and it was now that Livingston excelled themselves. In particular Horace Stoute – who played for the Barbados national side – stopped two St Johnstone penalties, and the away side ended up winning 4-2 in a dramatic shoot-out. It was a sweet moment in Livingston's early history and ensured Stoute – who was to leave at the end of the season – a permanent place in the hearts of Livingston fans. The cup run then ended with a 2-1 third round defeat at the hands of Partick Thistle at Meadowbank, but by now Livingston had at least begun to make some positive football headlines.

Slowly, the painful memories of the last two seasons and the bloody infighting at the club were beginning to fade and to be replaced with new memories.

The cup run, and especially the St Johnstone triumph, also showed how the new club could slowly develop its own, distinct identity. The club's connection with the traditions of Meadowbank and before that Ferranti had not been completely severed – the memories lived on in the hearts of men such as John Bain, Hugh Cowan and Bill Mill – but they had been altered. Now the new town club needed something it could call its own. Just about everyone connected with Livingston knew the size of the task they faced. A football club is more than simply a name, a ground and a team of players. What completes a club is its unique atmosphere, the character and devotion of its fans – and of course traditions. None of these can be invented overnight or simply added on like a coat of paint or a new layer of turf. They have to grow organically, with real passion and real feelings, and do not develop simply through the artificiality of a marketing campaign. That night at McDiarmid Park had now become part of the new Livingston's tradition, and was an authentic experience and a thrilling atmosphere. It was the first real step on the lengthy road to a real and living club history.

If the cup had shown glimpses of hope, it took longer for the club to come alive in the early league games, even though the performances themselves were encouraging. The problem was largely due to the fact they still had to play at Meadowbank; a major inconvenience that – thanks to yet more delays in completing the stadium at Almondvale – would last until November.

The first league game had been against Inverness Caledonian Thistle, the amalgamated team who had won admission to the Third Division from the Highland League and who had history with both Meadowbank and Ferranti. The West Lothian side won 3-0, though the Highland side would later get revenge in the second round of the Scottish Cup. Livingston continued their strong start to the Third Division campaign, and there was a certain irony in the fact that their first loss in the league was a 1-0 defeat at home to Arbroath; on the last occasion that the side played in the Commonwealth Stadium. Given the furore surrounding the club's departure from its old HQ, the result was somehow grimly appropriate: just 236 fans turned up to watch this sad end of an era. At the time, Jim Leishman wrote in Livingston's official publication, the Almondvale View: I would like to thank all the supporters that have watched us here. It will bring back some great memories for you, but it is time to move on to pastures new.

The next home game, however, would be played in an altogether different atmosphere. The first match for Livingston at their brand new Almondvale home was played on 11 November 1995 against East Stirling. The pessimists at Livingston had expected that around 1,000 fans would turn out to catch a first glimpse of the town's new senior side. The dark skies and pouring rain that greeted the historic day did not make the crowd forecasts any more hopeful. The people of Livingston and West Lothian were made of sterner stuff, however, and proved to be even more enthusiastic about senior football than the club had dared hope. A combination of the heavy rain and the large crowd in fact caused the kick-off to be delayed – by which time the newly-painted ground was full to capacity with 4,000 expectant fans. The atmosphere was electric, perhaps helped by the damp, close weather conditions. The game did not disappoint, even if the result was not quite perfect. In a seesawing affair, Livingston appropriately scored the first goal at the brand new stadium when Jason Young shot home to an ecstatic reaction from the home support. East Stirling, though, clearly had not read the script and equalised with 20 minutes to go. However, the draw barely dampened the enthusiasm of the supporters, nor of the Livingston officials. The day was a triumph for the new club, and in particular for the man who had fought to bring the club to West Lothian, Bill Hunter. For him above all it was an occasion to savour.

The rest of the season, too, was to be a good one for Hunter and the rest of the new club at Livingston. True, the desired first home win at

Almondvale was to prove a little elusive. The next home game saw Livingston lose 1-0 to Cowdenbeath and it was not until the New Year, on 10 January, that the new town team won in front of the Almondvale faithful, beating Queen of the South 3-1. In the Scottish Cup, victory over Stranraer in the first round was offset by a disappointing 3-2 loss away at Highland 'rivals' Inverness Caley (who to add insult to injury were later drawn against Rangers in a lucrative tie).

But the league was the real measure of success as far as this ambitious young club was concerned, and here the management and team did not disappoint. A consistent run of form saw Livingston threatening to achieve promotion in their first season. The crucial game was on 13 April, away at Brechin City, who were also seeking promotion. It was a curious replay of the situation in 1983 when Meadowbank Thistle had met the Glebe Park side, when both teams had also then been seeking promotion, in that case from the old Second Division. On that occasion a draw had been enough to win Brechin the championship title, and earn Thistle promotion for the first time in their history. Now, in 1996, former Dunfermline player Grant Tierney's solitary goal was enough to warn the points that guaranteed Livingston's promotion from the Third Division (Brechin were later to clinch promotion as well). A win over Arbroath then saw Livingston wrap up the championship title. It had been a remarkable, winning performance in their first (and so far only) season in the Third Division. Somehow the club had managed this despite the disruption of having to play back at the old Commonwealth Stadium for the first quarter of the season, and with all the tensions and confusion of moving to a new town and a new home base. The home support had been strong too, with an average gate of around 2,000. Events had vindicated Bill Hunter and his directors, who had been ridiculed for suggesting the new ground would attract even 1,500 for a home game.

Much of the credit for Livingston's footballing performance in 1995/96 must of course go to their manager Jim Leishman. Big Jim or 'The Bard' as he is sometimes known because of his penchant for writing verse, had been a legendary figure at Dunfermline, the club he had supported as a lad. As manager, Leishman (whose playing career had been cut short by injury) had driven the Pars up through the rungs of Scottish league football from the Second Division to the Premier division. Now, in his first full season in charge of Livingston, the colourful Leishman had already tasted success, thanks to his mixture of astute tactics and natural flair for man management and motivation. From the start, the backers of the

Livingston dream had promised that one day soon the club would make it into the top flight of Scottish football. They still had a long way to go, but Leishman had given them the ideal start; and as long as Big Jim remained in charge of the team, there was every hope the club may one day realise its ambitions.

If events on the field were going as well as anyone could have dared hope, the same could not be said for developments off the pitch. Financially, the club had been boosted by the increase in gate receipts caused by the growth in home support. In the year ending June 1996, the total revenue from Third Division matches at Almondvale was more than £75,000, a huge increase on the miserable £13,000 in gate income from the last full year at Meadowbank Stadium. In other respects, however, the financial outlook was much bleaker. The club had the laudable ambition to field full-time professionals and eventually field a fully professional side. This would, however, cost money in extra wages and signing-on fees, as well as the possibility of having to pay higher transfer fees. In the final season as Meadowbank Thistle the total bill for wages, national insurance and signing-on fees was just over £128,000. The bill for similar costs in the first year as Livingston more than doubled in size to £313,000. There was a similarly gloomy story elsewhere in the club's accounts. The cost of the move from Meadowbank had been considerable, with a number of extra expenses having to be absorbed by the club in the first year; there were for example the inevitable legal expenses for arranging the deal to the new town. The new stadium also bought higher fixed costs. This included the annual rental of the new stadium (leased a 125 year lease), which amounted to £30,000 and was calculated to rise as the club became more successful. The cost of heating and lighting meanwhile rose astronomically from just £621 at Meadowbank, to more than £30,000 at Almondvale. The cost of policing and stewards doubled to more than £17,000, while expenses for insurance, printing, administration, medical equipment and advertising also all saw huge increases. On the other side of the balance sheet, the defeat in the cup at the hands of Inverness Caley had meant the club brought in barely £630 from the competition in 1995/96; this contrasted rather starkly with the £80,000 earned the previous season thanks to the away tie at Celtic (Caley had of course gone on to draw Rangers). On the plus side donations and sponsorship had swelled the coffers by nearly £150,000, a ten-fold increase on the previous year's efforts. The overall outcome of this mixture of increased costs coupled with a (less pronounced) increase in income was a trading loss of £125,128 on gross income of £442,489. This contrasted with a £27,410 trading loss for the previous year on a turnover of £210,179. In short, the club's income had increased, but not as fast as it outgoings.

In the short term, this might not be a problem; after all the club was not likely to go through an expensive move again and an increase in costs had been expected. However, if the wage bill and other costs continued to grow, then here was a warning sign that financial obstacles could hold back the development of this forward-looking club.

The 1996/97 had a familiar feel to it. Back in the Second Division, and with its sights set firmly on the First division and beyond, Livingston more than held its own. With young striker Graham Harvey to the fore as top scorer (as he was for the next season too), the club was a fixture in the top half of the division. Frustratingly it finished in third spot and missed promotion after a weak finish to the season , but few doubted that under Leishman's control the side was continuing to make great strides. Only in the main cup competitions was there a sense of disappointment. In the League Cup Livingston were well beaten 5-2 away at Ayr in the first round, while in the Scottish Cup old league rivals Brechin abruptly stopped the club's progress in the second round. (Livingston's only knockout consolation that season was lifting the East of Scotland Cup.)

The failure to make an impact in the main cup competitions inevitably had an effect on the club's finances, which despite the best efforts of Bill Hunter and the board seemed to be getting worse by the month. This was not helped by the club's decision to build a new stand at the cost of £1million, the aim being to expand so that more fans could be housed in the future. The feeling was, among some observers, that the club needed to put itself on a sounder financial footing before similar ventures could be tried in the future. There was a danger that it was trying to spread its wings too fast, too far, and without the necessary strong monetary foundations. As it was the trading operating loss had roughly doubled in the following year (to June 1997) to around a quarter of a million pounds. Suddenly the finances of the club were beginning to look precarious.

Among those casting an anxious eye at the state of the club was the new West Lothian Council, the body that had taken over from the Lothian Region, the LDC and West Lothian district council. The WLC was as keen as anyone that Livingston FC should become a success for the new town. On the pitch and in the stands, the club was more than living up to its promise; the team had won promotion and already won a vociferous and loyal support from the town and the nearby area. Yet, for this success to be maintained and grown, the WLC wanted to be sure that Livingston had a long-term future in the area, and were not simply a short-term boost. In the words of one of those in the council at the time who was anxious about the club, Livingston had to be run on a modern, football business model, and 'not .....Sustained on the basis of periodic injections of cash from either individual investors or the local authority'. Much as they wanted the club in the area, councillors did not want to be left with a financial white elephant on their hands; and there seemed to be a danger that the finances at Livingston FC could be starting to unravel. One step taken in 1997 was the election of Tony Kinder, a senior councillor at West Lothian, to the club's board of directors. This move was to serve two related purposes; to safeguard the council's investment in the football club, and also to act as a sign of how important the authority regarded the club's presence in West Lothian.

The club itself was well aware of the problems it was facing, though this did not make the solution any easier. At the annual general meeting on 30 April 1997, chairman Bill Hunter praised the success of the football team, and singled out Jim Leishman for the work he had done to make the team competitive. But according to the minutes, Hunter, while still 'confident' about the future, admitted the club had been through a 'rough' year financially. The chairman then suggested the club needed new ideas and personnel if it were to move forward – and even hinted that he might be ready to leave the fray himself. As the minutes record: 'The Chairman made the point that no longer could the Club think in terms of the old Meadowbank days as this was now a vibrant thriving business we were trying to run and it was possible the existing Board would require [sic] to rethink their positions as it was necessary to bring in new faces who had both the expertise and financial backing to allow the club to progress.'

They added: 'The Chairman felt in his own case he might have to step aside to allow new blood into the organisation. The Chairman felt everyone associated with the Club should take pride in realising the achievements that had been made since the Meadowbank days, but reiterated fresh faces were necessary to move the Club forward to the next level.'

This was a major admission by Bill Hunter. For two years he had fought bitterly to bring the struggling Edinburgh club to West Lothian, and it was under two years since the club had set up home at Almondvale. Yet here was this most pugnacious and determined of characters suggesting he might retire into the background to let others lead the fight.

In fact, it was to be some time before Bill Hunter finally handed over the reins of power to others. In the meantime, Jim Leishman's team again started strongly in the Second Division in the 1997/98 season, with striker Graham Harvey scoring the goals at one end and future Celtic and Scotland goalkeeper Robert Douglas stopping them at the other. A home League Cup tie saw the club lose 2-0 to their former Edinburgh neighbours Hearts, but nearly 5,000 turned out to watch the game; the side was meanwhile unfortunate to lose 6-5 on penalties in the third round of the Scottish Cup against Albion Rovers after two draws. The manager was also pursuing a sensible long-term policy of finding and developing young players, so the club would be less reliant on imported and possibly more expensive players in the future. It was also a way of tapping into the football talent and enthusiasm that existed in West Lothian.

The grim financial situation, however, simply refused to go away and began to hang over the club like a low, dark cloud. As the 1997/98 season progressed, there was real concern from the local authority and others that unless action was taken soon, the club could collapse altogether. In the view of those at West Lothian at the time, the club was in danger of trading unlawfully, and also at risk of going into receivership. According to those same sources, it had cumulative debts of just over £1million, a sizeable amount of which was owed to the authority. Someone had to act, and act swiftly.

At about this time, club director and local councillor Tony Kinder received an interesting phone call. It was from Willie Haughey, the one-time director of Celtic, and he was keen to arrange a meeting. This meeting was to be between the pair of them, plus Dominic Keane, Haughey's friend and another former director at Parkhead. The council was understandably pleased at this turn of events, and was happy for Kinder to talk with the pair to see if there was a way that Livingston FC could be turned around. The two men had all the right credentials after all; knowledge of how to run a successful club, good business contacts and financial clout. They also shared a deep passion for football. The initial meeting between the three men went on for some hours. Later the trio adjourned for dinner at the prestigious Champany Inn, Linlithgow where over a meal of (very) well-done steak plus the unorthodox side dish (at least, at such an establishment) of baked beans, they discussed the future of Livingston FC. The news that Tony Kinder could provide about the real state of Livingston FC's finances were doubtless rather less digestible than the restaurant's cooking.

Kinder gave the inside track on what the authority was thinking. The council knew that as matters stood, the football club was unsustainable and it was not able or indeed inclined to offer unlimited and unconditional support. What the club desperately needed was a new team – not on the field of play, but in the boardroom. It needed some 'big hitters' to turn the club around. Both men would certainly answer to that description.

The two men had only recently left as directors at Celtic, both of them leaving after internal disputes when the leading figure at Parkhead was Fergus McCann. Haughey had been ousted and Keane, the Glasgow's club's respected secretary, had resigned on a point of principle. Departure from Parkhead for two such life-long Celtic fans had been, of course, a huge personal wrench. But it did mean that two 'big hitters' were now free to pursue their interest in football elsewhere. Now the two men were curious about the situation at this new club of Livingston that had so much potential; and the pair were now getting the full story of what the council and others thought about its prospects.

The meeting between Kinder, Keane and Haughey had not come out of the blue, however. Though the council had a crucial role in events, the initial approach to Willie Haughey and Dominic Keane had come from Bill Hunter himself. As the 1997/98 season proceeded, the Prestonpans businessman was more aware than ever that alone he could not rescue the club's fortunes. He knew it needed help from outside. Though the team was once more bidding strongly for promotion, the attendances were starting to drop from those of the previous two seasons. This was blamed on two factors. The poor, muddy state of the pitch had been a concern at Almondvale, leaving it even more vulnerable than most to the vagaries of Scottish weather. The postponement of some Saturday games had meant the re-arranged fixtures took place in midweek – when far fewer fans traditionally turned out. The second factor was the rise in fortune at Hearts that year; as a result of which fans from West Lothian were making the trip to the capital rather than staying at Almondvale. This saw the average gate at Livingston slump dramatically by a third to around 1,300. Such a drop in gate receipts was harming the club's already perilous financial situation.

So it was that in January 1998 Hunter revealed he would be willing to sell his controlling interest of shares in the club for the princely sum of £1. It may have looked strange economics at the time – Hunter had sunk around £140,000 into the club and would never see this money again – but there were good reasons for the offer. The businessman still believed in the vision of what he had helped to create, but was realistic enough to know that he lacked the resources to achieve success alone. To sell his controlling interest for a nominal sum would allow the new owners to put their cash where it was really needed – paying off club debts and investing in its future – rather than on a purchase fee. It would be a financial sacrifice for the chairman, but one he was willing to make for the sake of the club.

Haughey, the millionaire founder, and owner of Glasgow-based City Refrigeration's – a hugely successful facilities management business – had in fact rebuffed Hunter's initial approach. But now the former Celtic director's curiosity about Livingston had been tweaked. Together with Keane, a former Royal Bank of Scotland manager an astute financier, Haughey decided to take a closer look at Livingston.

Though the pair had been approached by a number of football clubs in trouble – and would be approached by even more when news of the Livingston negotiations leaked out – they were particularly intrigued by Livingston. The club had a new name and a new fan base and a great potential to grow into its West Lothian surroundings. The two found it tempting. Another player in this 'consortium' was their friend and lottery winner John McGuinness. McGuinness, another passionate Celtic fan who had bought shares in the Glasgow club from Haughey, had previously considered taking a stake in Livingston when the financial plight of the club had first become known and after Bill Hunter had hinted at the 1997 AGM he might step aside. At the time he had decided against it because, as he says, 'I'd been through their accounts!'. Now that his two friends Haughey and Keane were involved, both men who knew how a football club should be run, McGuinness was this time tempted to become involved.

Negotiations were quickly under way early in 1998, and Hunter was as good as his word in agreeing to handover his controlling interest in the Second Division club for £1. By 12 March the deal was effectively done, though it still had to be formally ratified the following month at the club's annual general meeting.

Under the terms of the deal, Hunter reduced his number of the shares from 72 per cent to some eleven per cent, giving the new team effective control of the club. The former Prestonpans builder also agreed to step down as chairman – to be replaced by Tony Kinder – though he was to stay on as a non-executive director. Meanwhile the new management team poured in an immediate £200,000 to shore up the club's finances, and promised a fresh series of investments for the future, including a fourth stand and a new playing surface. Haughey's major role was to lend the club an estimated £1million in an interest free loan (a sum that has since been repaid, ending Haughey's links with the club). The new hands-on boss at the club was to be Dominic Keane, whose experience as club secretary at Celtic had given him powerful insight into the running of a football club. At the same time the former Celtic manager David Hay, one of the great names of Scottish football, had been brought on board as a consultant.

So a bloodless coup at Livingston had taken place, with barely a whisper or a murmur of disapproval. Out had gone Bill Hunter, the man who had carried the burden of moving the old Meadowbank to a new town and to a new and better future. In had come a team who, with the right resources and knowledge of football at the top, had every chance of helping the club fulfil its dreams.

Speaking at the time, Bill Hunter acknowledged that he had had little realistic choice over selling the club if he wanted to see it survive and one-day flourish. He said: 'it was a sacrifice I was prepared to make to get the club back on a sound financial footing. It is better having an 11 per cent stake in something rather than a 72 per cent stake in nothing.'

Hunter added: 'I still believe this club will be playing in the Premier League because the potential is enormous.'

Later, when he resigned as a director in the summer, Bill Hunter admitted it was tough to say goodbye to the club. 'I am obviously sorry to leave the club after such a long time. I wish the new men in charge all the best and I hope they can complete the job I started.'

That 'job' had started back in 1991 when the former benefactor of Meadowbank Thistle had finally joined the board, and then taken control of the club over the following two years. Hunter had presided over – indeed instigated – the audacious move away from the club's old base at the Commonwealth Stadium in Edinburgh to its new West Lothian home. Though bitterly attacked for the decision by a small but vociferous group of Thistle fans, Hunter had insisted it had been the right move. Left in Edinburgh, with just a few hundred fans for company, Meadowbank had threatened to fade slowly and quietly away into oblivion. With the new identity the club now had a fresh start and the chance to build its own unique and much larger fan base. Unfortunately, the businessman's determination to make the club succeed in Livingston was not enough. Turning fully professional, and aiming to provide First Division and Premier League standards, the club had been under-capitalised. Hunter had lacked the financial clout to take Livingston onto its next stage as a sustainable, growing club that could not just survive – but prosper in higher divisions. But as those who remained at Livingston knew well, without Bill Hunter's vision in the first place, the club would never have had the chance to fulfil its potential.

The Hunter era was over, and the new management team was taking his place, but there was no time for a honeymoon period. For one thing, Keane and the others had to come to terms with the reality of the financial problems the club faced. At the time, it was unable to pay its employees, the bank, its suppliers or its taxes. 'It was pretty bust,' Keane later admitted. There was also the small matter of getting promotion. For the club to have a long-term financial future in West Lothian and attract the sort of fan base it needed to succeed, the club needed to move out of the Second Division. Right until the end of the season it had looked as if Livingston would not just gain promotion, but win the title as well. With the final game beckoning, and with the West Lothian side at home, the dream of making it to the First Division seemed all but certain to come true.

Unfortunately for them, the visitors were Inverness Caley, a side with whom they had had some famous tussles, and a team that was in the mood to spoil the home team's party. In a shock result the Highland side won 2-1, and with the turn of events elsewhere, Stranraer and Clydebank managed to shove Livingston into third place and out of the promotion spots. The outcome was a bitter blow for the new regime at the club. Dominic Keane was distraught, even though his beloved Celtic won the Premier League on the same day; Big Jim Leishman was so upset he even considered quitting the game. (To make matters worse, the championship trophy had actually been brought to the ground that day, so convinced were the authorities that they would be handing it over to Livingston that season – it was something the superstitious Keane would not allow to happen again.) For the disconsolate fans, there was more perplexing news to come.

The failure to win promotion, when it had seemed all but certain, had been a blow not just for morale but for the club's future expansion. First Division football would have meant bigger gates, more sponsorship and stronger finances. So if the club could not (as yet) get promoted to First Division football, why not buy it? This seemed the reasoning behind the news that Livingston was now talking with officials at newly promoted First Division club Clydebank about a merger. On one level it seemed perfect; the Bankies were homeless, the Lions without First Division football. Bringing the new merged club to the West Lothian Courier

Stadium at Almondvale (and still calling the club Livingston) would solve both problems. However, the Clydebank fans were furious at the news and insisted they would never accept it. The Livingston fans meanwhile seemed more bemused than angry. Peter Gough, chairman of the official Livingston Supporters Club, said: 'this has all happened without any of us knowing about it. .... I do feel sorry for Clydebank and I'd like to let them know that we have had nothing to do with this.'

In the event, the Livingston's fans' sympathy was not necessary as the plan fell by the wayside and the West Lothian side had to prepare for another season in the Second Division. The proposed plan had however shown not just that Scottish football clubs, many of whom were in poor financial shape, were willing to try new structures and ideas to improve their lot; but also that the new Keane regime at Livingston was desperately, impatiently ambitious for the club.

This ambition was soon exhibited in happier ways, as far as the fans were concerned, during the close season. In a massive changeover of personnel, familiar names such as Graham Harvey left the club, while no fewer than thirteen new faces arrived. Of these the star name was without doubt the Hearts star striker John Robertson, who at the age of 33 and in the twilight of his playing career, was now seeking fresh challenges. He was appointed player-coach. Robertson already had family connections with the club; as a boy John had been a ball boy at Meadowbank Thistle's first competitive match in 1974. A decade later his older brother Chris had been Thistle's stop scorer in their first season of First Division football; now John was hoping to inspire the Thistle's heirs at Livingston back into the First Division. Other new signings included the former Dunfermline striker David Bingham, Brian McPhee, Sean Sweeney and former Hamilton midfielder Jim Sherry, who was to become captain. Off the pitch, Jim Leishman had been made general manager of the club – effectively Dominic Keane's right-hand man – to produce a root-and branch reform of the club's football structures and to prepare it for higher league football. His place as manager was taken by former Scotland international Ray Stewart. With David Hay already in place, Livingston now had the strongest management and playing team in its history so far (either as Thistle or the Lions), and showed just how far the new owners of the club were prepared to go to achieve success. The next few seasons promised to be exhilarating times for Livingston fans.

The 1998/99 season was noteworthy for two key reasons. Livingston knocked Aberdeen out of the Scottish Cup (winning away 1-0) and, more importantly for its long-term plans, finally won promotion to the First Division at the third attempt. They were indeed promoted as champions. Not surprisingly, with top players on show, and with a run of fine performances to enjoy, the crowds grew as well, the average attendances nearly doubling to 2,500. The new signings mostly proved very shrewd, with Robertson playing in 36 leagues games and becoming top scorer, while Bingham was the top marksman in the next two seasons.

The following season saw the club make an assault on its ultimate ambition and a place in the Premier League for the first time in its history. The bold attempt fired the West Lothian public as the club averaged nearly 4,000 per home gate; in the event, the club fell a few points short of their dream and finished in fourth place. However, this was still a creditable effort from a club that had languished in the Third Division just a few seasons before. It also made the management team realise what it would take to make that final stretch for glory. The next season, 2000/01, was to be the one where the dream was finally achieved.

The omens had been good for the season when Livingston embarked on a fantastic run on the Scottish Cup, in which they beat East Fife, Aberdeen again (1-0 in a lucrative replay away)and then Peterhead in an improbable quarter-final. The semi-final at Hampden Park against old Edinburgh rivals Hibernian was something of a return to reality in which they lost 3-0, though receipts from the crowd of nearly 25,000 helped cushion the blow. In any case, the team had clearly got the taste for the football good life, and saw promotion to the Premier League as their way of achieving it. A fantastic run of results saw the Lions leading the pack at the top of the First Division; and with three games they had the chance to clinch promotion. Their opponents, inevitably give the two club's recent rivalries, were Inverness Caley and the Livingston team and supporters travelled north on the A9 feeling a heady mixture of excitement, anticipation and nerves. The game was every bit as nerve-wracking as the long journey up. Once again, Caley were rightly determined to do their best to ruin the West Lothian side's party, as they had in the Second Division back in 1998. The away fans' worst fears were then confirmed when Paul Sheerin opened the scoring for the Highland side after just 17 minutes. Were the nightmares of 1998 returning to haunt Keane, Leishman and the rest of the club once more? However, the Livingston contingent's nerves were calmed when new signing star striker David Fernandez scored fifteen minutes later, and their anxiety turned to delight when Barry Wilson put the Lions ahead with a penalty just before half-time. Livingston's happiness was complete ten minutes after the break when, under pressure from Fernandez, Caley defender Stuart McCaffrey unluckily diverted the ball into his own net. The score was 3-1; Livingston were finally heading for the SPL. Even a last-minute penalty by Sheerin, making the final score 3-2, could not dampen the joy of the Livingston players, fans – and officials.

It was official – Livingston were promoted to the Premier League. In doing so they had achieved the remarkable, and unique, feat of moving up through all divisions of Scottish football – from the Third Division to the SPL. Not surprisingly, surveying the fans and the players' reactions, Jim Leishman and Dominic Keane were ecstatic.

Leishman described the moment as one of the proudest of his life and added: 'we have made history by being the first club to come up from the Third Division to the SPL. It is some achievement. Livingston are going places.'

Meanwhile, talking to the overjoyed Livingston fans at the ground, chairman Dominic Keane was in ebullient mood. 'This shows it's not all negatives in football,' he declared. 'Three years ago when I took over, there was no money at the club and now we're in the Premier League. We're now just starting and it's a long road. We're writing the history books as we go along. I'm making no predictions. The bottom line is, we're there.'

It was a proud moment for the Livingston club who, as Keane pointed out, had been close to going under a few years before. When he, McGuinness and Haughey had taken control of the club in 1998, they had conceived a five-year plan to get into the SPL. They had now achieved it in three – and also now had a 10,000-seat ground to set the seal on their new status.

As well as looking forward to the challenges ahead, though, it was also a time to reflect on the past. Thirty years before, the club – then the former parks and welfare league team Ferranti Thistle – had been playing in the East of Scotland League and had not even entered the Scottish Cup. There was little or no money around in those days; their manager at the time John Bain recalls 'selling' a player to Stirling Albion in return for a football. Bain had then helped to take the club as Meadowbank Thistle into the Scottish League and a new era had begun. Though eventually making it to the First Division under the management of Terry Christie, Thistle had struggled to succeed off the field in the shadow of the well-supported Hearts and Hibs clubs in the capital. In a bold move, Bill

Hunter had relocated the club from Edinburgh to West Lothian, changing its name to Livingston en route. Hunter had not been able to see the club achieve its dream, and beset by financial problems it had come close to ruin; but in the new era of Dominic Keane and his colleagues Livingston had finally fulfilled that dream. The battle to reach the Premier League had been a difficult, sometimes painful but always exciting journey. Yet in many ways this extraordinary ascent to the summit of Scottish football had come about remarkably quickly. As John Bain, now an Honorary Vice President of Livingston noted: 'If I close my eyes I can still see the days where we played on public parks.'

Since its arrival in the SPL, Livingston has worked hard to retain its new-found reputation as one of Scotland's top football clubs. It had battled hard to get where it was, at the expense of much blood, sweat tears – and not a little money – and was not going to surrender its status easily. The icing on the cake for many Livingston fans was the club's astonishing first season in the SPL, when the West Lothian club finished third in the division, with just the Old Firm pair or Celtic and Rangers above them. This of course led to yet another level of success that had seemed unimaginable when men such as John Bain and another Honorary Vice-President Bill Mill had been together in the old Ferranti days: European football.

To the delight of all at the club, its third table position had qualified Livingston to take part in the 2002/03 UEFA Cup.

The first European match in its club history was a qualifying two-leg contest against the Liechtenstein side Vaduz; the first leg was away on Tuesday, 13 August. Around 300 loyal Lions fans made the journey out to watch the historic encounter, and were rewarded with a hard-earned 1-1 draw against the part-time but determined Liechtenstein team. A goalless draw back at Livingston ensured the Scottish side progressed through to the first round proper of the UEFA Cup – another first for the club. Here the West Lothian side met the decidedly useful Austrian side Sturm Graz, in what proved to be a lively pair of games. The first, played at the delightfully-named Arnold Schwarzenegger Stadium in Graz, ended with the home side winning 5-2; the return game at Almondvale saw an even more remarkable game as Livingston ran out 4-3 winners on the night. The aggregate was an incredible 8-6 to the Austrian side, but Livingston had not been disgraced. They had at least exited their first European campaign with something of a flourish.

As with any football club, changes have continued to occur at

Livingston. Players from all around the world continue to come and go at the club, providing new skills and excitement for the fans; at the same time the club has started ambitious plans to develop its own youth players, as well as being a feeder club for the world's most glamorous club Manchester United. Big Jim Leishman, who during eight-and-a-half wonderfully committed years was variously manager, general manager, chief executive and manager again, has finally left to return to his first true love in football – Dunfermline Athletic. Nonetheless, 'Leish', as he is popularly known, will always be remembered for his part in Livingston's incredible rise from the Third Division.

Meanwhile in June 2003, Livingston showed their ambition by appointing as head coach Marcio Maximo – the first Brazilian to occupy such a position in a Scottish club.

Such innovation should perhaps come as no surprise that Livingston have once more broken the mould. Since its formation as Ferranti Thistle after the end of the Second World War, the club has always done things differently, and sometimes the hard way. Twice it has changed its name, and three times its home ground. Along the way it has attracted some hurtful jokes and bitter criticism, some of it almost too much to bear. But at the same time the club had won friends (as well as championships) for its honest attempts to do better, for the way it has overcome adversity and setbacks to become the club it has today. Throughout it all, the club has tried to maintain a family atmosphere, for all its domestic fall-outs and rows. Livingston FC stands today as the true heirs of Ferranti Thistle and Meadowbank Thistle; standing proud among the best clubs in Scotland. The dream of John Bain and so many others have finally come true amid the glamour of Premier League football. Not bad indeed for a parks team.

9

THE FANS

THE FANS ARE THE MAGIC ingredients of any football club. They do not just help pay the players' wages or keep the club afloat financially – though no finance director would doubt that important role. They are essential in establishing a club's identity. Indeed, in many respects the fans *are* the club. Managers come and go, so too do star players. The fans, however, stay with the club, through the good times, and the more frequent bad times. They are the constant, eternal factor in the ever-changing world of football.

In the case of Livingston FC, however, the story is made a little more complicated. The club has enjoyed no fewer than three different identities since it was formed back in 1943 (Ferranti, Meadowbank and Livingston), and has regarded as home some four separate grounds. Few clubs can boast such a colourful and varied history in such a relatively short period, and few sets of supporters have had to face the challenges that have beset those of this club. Yet while they may not always have been great in number, the supporters have always made up for it with fierce loyalty, humour – and not a little eccentricity. The current Livingston fans are therefore heirs to a fine tradition.

The very first Ferranti Thistle fans were, of course, a small but select group of people. The windswept ground at Crewe Toll, which sat conveniently next to the main Ferranti factory, was not designed for comfort or for vast crowds. This was just as well. As the Thistle side ploughed its way (sometimes literally) through the mud in welfare leagues and then from 1953 in the East of Scotland, sometimes only a handful of supporters would turn up to watch. On good days it might be fifty. Often those patrolling the touchlines were colleagues of the players in the works team side, or friends, wives, girlfriends or relatives. Very often too they would be members of the Ferranti (Edinburgh) Recreation Club who used the site, and out of whose belly the football club had been spawned. Sometimes senior executives from the company would also turn up to lend support for the team that bore the company's name. A keen follower of football in general, and Thistle in particular, was the one-time general manager of the company in Scotland John (later Sir John) Toothill. He had a good working relationship with manager John Bain and saw as many games as the demands of work would allow. Not all senior executives were such great football fans, however. The general manager from 1968 to 1985 Sir Donald McCallum has admitted he was not a regular at the Crewe Toll ground though he did watch the side on at least one occasion. . He told the author: 'I must confess that football is not my game and my main memory is of being jolly cold!' Nevertheless, despite his lack of enthusiasm for the beautiful game, Sir Donald – in common with all Ferranti bosses – always helped the club in any way he could.

At the end of the Sixties, when redevelopment at Crewe Toll forced Thistle to move, the club relocated to the nearby ground at Pilton, known as City Park. This was what might be called a 'proper' football pitch, one that had once played host to senior league and cup football when the old Edinburgh United played there. (They have since reformed and now play at Meadowbank Stadium – Thistle's next ground.) The more accessible nature of City Park ensured that Thistle home games attracted more fans than before. Some were simply curious at this works team that were playing to a high standard in the respected east of Scotland League; others saw it as a more restful place to watch football than the frenetic noise of Easter Road or Tynecastle. As an added attraction, it also had an eccentrically sloping playing surface (as indeed did Easter Road). Whatever the fans' motives for attending, they were usually rewarded with some entertaining play as Thistle's manager John Bain – who had been in charge since 1953 – was an advocate of open, attacking football. The attendances were reasonable for the East of Scotland League; for routine home matches perhaps as many as 200 came to watch Thistle play.

The crowds inevitably increased in size once the carrot of Scottish Cup football was dangled in front of them. Ferranti were only allowed to become full members of the Scottish Football Association (and thus play in the cup) after the authorities forced them to fence in an open part of the ground at City Park. Apparently, the SFA had visions of thousands of marauding fans rampaging out of control as Thistle took on the likes of Hawick Royal Albert, Civil Service Strollers, or perhaps Brechin City. Thistle's first Scottish Cup match was a first round tie against Duns in 1972 which, depending on whose version you believe, attracted either a disappointing crowd of 150, or the distinctly impressive figure of 1,000. However many were present, the result is not in dispute, and a 3-1 home win saw Thistle's fans enjoy their biggest game so far – a home tie in the second round against Elgin City. The atmosphere at this match was a special one and certainly very noisy, a far cry from Thistle's usual loyal but muted support. The drawn game meant a replay away to the Highland League side, and for the first time a sizeable contingent of Thistle fans travelled away to watch this side. This select band included the now former general manager Sir John Toothill who flew up to watch the game in an executive jet, thoughtfully taking manager John Bain with him. Among all the complaints at the time about long journeys to play or watch Highland League, this was clearly the only way to travel. Though most Thistle fans did not have the benefit of jets to fly them to matches, the presence of so many away fans at this game did mark an important breakthrough for the club. At long last, Ferranti Thistle fans were, literally, on the move. The next season the trend became even stronger. A cup-tie away at First Division side Partick Thistle was the incentive, and the club wisely laid on a small fleet of subsidised-fare coaches to take the fans to Firhill. Though the non-leaguers were well beaten, the several hundred Thistle fans made their noisy and enthusiastic mark on the day's events.

The metamorphosis from Ferranti Thistle to Meadowbank Thistle and the arrival of senior league football paradoxically underlined the extent to which the club's support was still largely based on the Ferranti Company. A system was set up for fans of the club who worked for the company to have a small sum – 5 pence – deducted each week to help keep the new semi-professional league team balance the books. Several hundred joined this bold scheme. Meanwhile the club attracted some 500 Founder Members who all contributed money to Thistle – many though not all of these members were Ferranti staff. Yet, though – at the bovine insistence of the Scottish League – Ferranti Thistle had to drop the company's name, the general reaction to this shortsighted decision was muted. This was possibly because the small band of fans was so excited at the breathtaking speed with which their team had gained league status; they were prepared to accept the inconvenience of having to shout out another name. At least they could still cheer on 'Thistle'.

The move to league status also meant yet another new ground – the Commonwealth Stadium. It was to be the butt of much humour over the 21 years that Meadowbank played at the ground. If City Park had been a little small, shabby, but loveable football ground, Meadowbank Stadium was a large, well-kept but unlovable athletics stadium. The 'concrete lavvy pan' was just one of the expressions used to describe it – and that was by home fans as well. The main stand's remoteness from the playing surface meant that rarely, if ever, did home games have that intensity of mood and emotion that smaller, purpose-built football grounds have (and which fans love). There was more than one reference to the moon (or various other non-terrestrial bodies) having more atmosphere than the Meadowbank Stadium.

If the Thistle fans were to develop their own brand of humour (much of it black) this probably owes everything to the club's disastrous start in second Division football in 1974/75. The opening home game against Albion Rovers had attracted – thanks to the allure of free programmes and a 'go-go' girl – around 4,000 curious spectators. By the time the club was well into its opening run of 14 straight defeats this was dipping as low as 300.

It has to be said that from day one (or day two if we consider the Albion game a relative success) Thistle singularly failed to capture the imagination of the Edinburgh football-going population. They were to continue to fail to capture it until the moment they left in 1995. Very little or perhaps none of this can be blamed on Meadowbank as a club; they tried to play attractive football and in later years the part-timers often punched well above their weight in terms of league status and giant-killing cup performances. The problem was that in a modestly sized city such as Edinburgh there were already two giants in the forest, Hibernian and Hearts. It was next to impossible for any other club to flourish in the shadow they cast.

Meadowbank's poor start to league football did at least have one very curious effect as far as their support went. It probably started with a television report; ITV's *World of Sport* ran a story on Meadowbank's dismal start to the season (five defeats in the League Cup, nine in the league, no draws, no wins). Now the outside sporting world was looking on in a kind of horrified awe at the Edinburgh side's run of defeats, and wondering if it could continue. Of course, it did not. On the very day of the much-watched TV report, Brechin City earned themselves the unenviable footnote in Scottish football history of becoming the first team to fail to beat Meadowbank Thistle in a competitive match. Even worse, the Glebe Park team actually *lost* to Thistle – and at home, too. The narrow but historic 1-0 win was the catalyst for celebrations in some unlikely spots around the country. Sports fans who had empathised with the new club's plight now drank toasts to the great victory. For many this was simply a bit of harmless fun, an example of the usual British trait of supporting the underdog. But for many, these events sparked the beginning of a genuine devotion to the club. Gradually over the next few years, and all over Britain, Meadowbank Thistle supporter's clubs began to emerge. There was also, by the beginning of the 1980's, a number of celebrity fans who had come out of the football closet and publicly 'confessed' that they were Thistle devotees. Suddenly, and much to the club's bemusement, Meadowbank Thistle were cool.

One of these celebrity fans was the rock star Rick Wakeman. Wakeman was and remains a committed football fan. His first love is Manchester City. However he, like many other English football fans, was transfixed by Thistle's run of bad form, and then equally delighted when they finally managed that tumultuous win at Brechin. Wakeman recalls: 'I took a few friends out and I toasted Meadowbank thistle all night with Famous Grouse and lager! From that moment on I followed everything they did and they became my "Scottish" team.'

Wakeman then describes how he kept faith with the club and later went to see them play.

'When my daughter [Jemma] was born in 1983 at Simpson's [Maternity Hospital] in Edinburgh I went to loads of games, the low point losing 2-1 at home to Elgin city in the cup [1982, first round]. I got to meet the manager, Terry Christie, the chairman [John Blacklaw] and other Thistle dignitaries and they were just so in love with the club it was infectious.

'When my daughter was born about fifteen guys from the supporters club were waiting at the hospital and presented my daughter with a doll dressed in Meadowbank colours. The doll was named Footy and I think it is still around. From that moment on, Jemma has been a supporter – although she has yet to see a game!'

Wakeman says he is 'thrilled' at the club's success since moving to Livingston, even though he admits to thinking of them still as 'Thistle'. He adds: 'It was a great re-location and an example to many other clubs. I shall be following their every move.'

He was by no means the only big name who had fallen in love with Thistle. Another was John Peel, the Radio One DJ and well-known Liverpool fan. Peel began to take an interest in Meadowbank Thistle when a listener suggested that if he was ever in Edinburgh he should drop by the Commonwealth Stadium to see Thistle play. In fact, the first time he watched the club was when they played Queen's Park over at Hampden. Interviewed in *The Weekly News* in 1983, the DJ remembered: 'when we got to Hampden, it was an amazing sight to see 300 people in a stadium that size. It wasn't a case of opposing supporters chucking bricks together, but huddling together for warmth!'

Peel was also quick to discern the legendary humour of the Thistle fans, and especially their chants. The best know of these was the immortal: 'Give us a, F, give us an I, give us an S, give us an L – what does that spell? THISTLE!'

Other well-known 'Fisl' fans included the newsreader Reginald Bosanquet and comic Stanley Baxter.

Some observers were critical of the celebrities' support for Thistle, describing it as an 'affectation' or even patronising. In his 1983 interview, Peel said he was irritated by such criticism. 'I admit it got to me because I live in Suffolk and it's a bit of a trek to Meadowbank, especially since I don't like flying,' he said. 'But what I've taken to doing is arranging discos at universities and clubs in Edinburgh which coincide with Meadowbank's home games – that way I've managed to see them about ten times so far.'

Peel added: 'I go to see Meadowbank because I enjoy it. From meeting the supporters in the pub across the road to sitting in the stand with them watching the game.'

Thistle's then manager Terry Christie also defended the celebrity fans at the time. 'The interest in us from people like Rick Wakeman and John Peel isn't just a pose by them. Rick was sitting in the boardroom after the cup-tie against Elgin with a Meadowbank scarf around his neck. He knew all about the players.

'John Peel too is a very down-to-earth bloke. He usually comes up and sits in the stand with the rest of our supporters and often doesn't even come into the boardroom afterwards.'

The unexpected support was not restricted to well-known figures, however. Supporter's clubs sprang up all over Britain, and especially in England. The biggest was the London supporters club, of which Reggie Bosanquet was honorary president, and which at its peak had some 200 members. (Bosanquet may have been joking, but in 1980 he said he was sure that the club would be in the Premier League by the year 2000; he was wrong, but only by a year – Livingston were promoted to the SPL in 2001.) Around 30 from the group would regularly make the long trek up from London to watch Thistle play at home. The supporters club called themselves the 'Cockney Thistles', designed and wore their own badge, and wrote their own newsletter. Even more remarkably, a blind fan and his wife from Epsom, Surrey, also often travelled up to watch Thistle play – and for some away matches as well as home games.

Other groups were based in Leeds, Merseyside, Braintree in Essex, Southampton Belfast, and Birmingham. Nigel Dowey, who in 1980 was treasurer of the Trinity and All Saints Colleges branch in Leeds, explained the appeal of the club at that time. 'They always had a certain charisma. And they never seemed very successful, so we thought we would back them. It was really through television that we became familiar with them.'

The supporters who did make it up from England were often offered hospitality in the boardroom. But John Blacklaw, chairman of the club from 1974 to 1992, admitted he was not sure for the club's widespread appeal. Speaking in 1983, when the far-flung support was at its peak, he said: 'If I knew the reason I'd be the best publicist in the country. I suppose it has something to do with the fact that we are the youngest club in the Scottish League. We are also a small outfit playing in a big ground, Meadowbank Stadium, where everyone is seated. But I still find it quite unbelievable that so many people in Britain are interested in us.'

The fans were welcome, nonetheless. Though the wags were not quite right – English fans did not yet outnumber the Scottish ones – attendances remained stubbornly low during the 1980's and early 1990's. This was despite the unusual step of Meadowbank allowing women free entry to the ground. The idea went back to the early days of Meadowbank Thistle and was the brainchild of Blacklaw himself; the chairman wanted to create a 'family' atmosphere at the club that would fit in with the 'family' ethos of the old Ferranti club and company. The chairman reckoned that encouraging more women fans by allowing them in free of charge would both engender a family feeling and perhaps reduce the prevalence of bad language and any violence. Certainly, over the years, the small Thistle faithful had a reputation for being well behaved, humorous and disinclined to violence.

However, they were also fiercely loyal – and the arrival of Bill Hunter at the club in 1991 and his later decision to move it to Livingston provoked a hard core of fans into a bitter reaction. The 'Battle of Meadowbank' undoubtedly tarnished the reputation of the club and it lost some of the aura of gentlemanly calm of the Blacklaw era. Some of the abuse aimed at Bill Hunter, and particularly his wife and daughter, went beyond the acceptable boundaries of protest; as did threatening messages to the businessman's home. On the other side, the way some loyal and law-abiding fans were treated during the episode (some were ejected and banned, and the officials supporters club not recognised) was heavy-handed and lacking in understanding. The fans had every right to feel aggrieved at the loss of the club's name and its relocation (though few truly mourned the loss of the 'concrete lavvy'), even if the level of protest sometimes went too far.

The result, inevitably, was that only a few Thistle fans transferred their loyalty to the club's new incarnation as Livingston FC. In any case one of the main reasons for moving to West Lothian was to tap into a new and predominantly young population, and one that was also lacking its own senior league side to support. The new club made sure that the West Lothian population were fully aware of the football teams imminent arrival in 1995. Pupils from St Margaret's High School in Livingston were bussed in to the Commonwealth Stadium when Thistle were still playing there. The aim was to encourage links between the new and old clubs. Meanwhile a marketing campaign was started in Livingston itself to publicise the club. In reality, though, the club was pushing at an open door. Though the area had many good and popular junior clubs, there had been no senior side to support. While many from West Lothian did travel to Glasgow and Edinburgh to watch Rangers, Celtic, Hearts and Hibernian, this was expensive, and getting more so every year.

The fact that the kick off for the first match at the brand new Almondvale stadium in November 1995 had to be delayed – while a capacity 4,000 crowd squeezed into their seats – was evidence enough of the potential support in the area. Inevitably, a full house did not turn up every week, and in the low point of the 1997/98 season the average attendance fell to around 1,300. But even this was nearly 500 more than the record average gate at Meadowbank (848 in 1988/89). In following seasons the figure touched 4,000, while since joining the SPL Livingston have attracted average home gates of between six and seven thousand. In terms of figures of fans alone, the move to West Lothian has been a massive success.

Slowly, too, the Livi fans have begun to build up their traditions and develop their own folklore. The first occasion when the Livingston tradition came alive was in the autumn of 1995, before the new club had even been able to move into its home at Almondvale (because of delays it was not ready till November). A band of hardy souls from the town made the journey up to Perth to watch the side take on St Johnstone in the second round of the League Cup. In theory the Third Division outfit should not have had much of a chance against the stronger McDiarmid Park side. Yet with the scores level after extra time, the tie went to penalties. It was at this moment that Livingston's goalkeeper Horace Stoute stepped forward to become a hero, saving two of the home side penalties and ensuring the West Lothian team won 4-2 in the shoot-out. Those fans who were present had seen a little moment of history; and the dawn of a new football heritage. Stoute – the Barbadian national keeper – became the first of the fans' heroes at the club. Many more have followed since; Graham Harvey, John Roberston, Jim Sherry, Paul 'Deasel' Deas, David Fernandez, Francisco Cabrera Guinovart ('Quino') among others.

Moreover, now that Livingston FC has been based at Almondvale for a number of years, a new generation of fans is growing up with fond memories of supporting Livi in their childhood.

One story comes from a Livi fan called 'Hack' who recalls his experience when he was just ten and the West Lothian gained promotion from the Third Division in their first season (1995/96). He says: 'The next week the Livi bus did a tour of West Lothian and me and a few mates went to the chip shop in Linlithgow to see it go past as that was the nearest place to Winchburgh (where I live). We ran out of the shop as we saw the bus go past and it pulled in to the bus stop opposite the chippy. They invited us on.

'For three 10 year olds this was great – amongst our favourite players. As the bus went along we hoped it would go through Winchburgh and drop us off.

'When we got to Winchburgh it just got better. As we were getting off the bus Big Jim shouted that they needed a rest from touring and that all the staff, players and fans on the bus should get off and go into the Tally Ho at the top of Winchburgh.

'This was great for us getting to spend more time with the Livi . . . in the Tally we got the trophy to hold proper and the manager of the month award, which was bloody heavy!'

These sort of experiences can stay with young fans for life, and encourage loyalty to a club. The treks to Europe, in particular the three-day journey that some fans took to get to watch Livi play Sturm Graz in Austria, have now inspired similar memories.

There is also still a connection between the club's identities of the past and now. There has, for example, long been rivalry between Thistle/Livi fans and those from Highland clubs, and especially from Inverness. As Ferranti, the club was involved in a fierce but friendly Scottish Cup tussle with Elgin City as long ago as 1972. The rivalry got rather less friendly after 1974 when to the shock of all of the Highland League, Ferranti Thistle were elected to the Scottish League ahead of Inverness Thistle. Thereafter the Highland fans let the Thistle team and supporters know exactly what they thought of this whenever their paths crossed; the fact that Ferranti had changed their name to Meadowbank made no difference to them. In particular Scottish Cup trips to Inverness Caledonian in 1978 and to Buckie Thistle two years later saw the Edinburgh contingent suffer plenty of taunting from the home support. The rivalry has survived, though with less hostility, into the Livingston era and after the two Inverness sides merged to form Inverness Caledonian Thistle or Caley as they are often known; the sides have met in some crucial end-of-season battles.

It was always going to be a formidable achievement to place an existing league club into another community with little time to prepare for the consequences. In the event, the experiment has proved astonishingly successful. The club now has a home it can call its own, and an area with which it can identify. For their part the West Lothian community has now found a senior football club to be proud of and through whom it can express its identity. They say that every football club gets the fans it deserves; eventually, and many years after it began life on the public parks, that can truly be said of Livingston.

POSTSCRIPT: CHANGE AND CONTINUITY

THE JOURNEY FROM FERRANTI THISTLE to Livingston FC, via Meadowbank, has not always been an easy one. Football, like most sports, tends to be conservative and this is no less true of football fans. They often frown upon changes. And undoubtedly this club – which has experienced three different names and even more different venues – has undergone more change than most in Scottish football. It is indeed hard, at first glance, to see much common ground between Ferranti Thistle and Livingston.

Yet looking back at the club, and its origins as a work team for the Ferranti Company, it is possible to pick out a thread of continuity with the current day. Inevitably, this continuity revolves around people.

The two honorary vice-presidents at Livingston, John Bain and Bill Mill, are both men with long service to the club dating far back into the Ferranti era. John Bain joined the Ferranti team when it played in the local welfare leagues and just before it joined the East of Scotland League in 1953. He became the club's first manager in that league, and was also in charge of the team in 1974 when it joined the Scottish League as Meadowbank Thistle; he is a regular at Livingston's home matches and even went to watch Livingston's away tie in Austria against Sturm Graz in the UEFA Cup.

Bill Mill joined the Ferranti Company in 1951. He had hoped for a career as a footballer but a leg injury in 1947 had ended that ambition. Instead, he joined the works team and later became secretary and treasurer of the club. Later, for a brief period in the early 1990s, Mill was chairman of Meadowbank Thistle.

Another veteran of the old days is the former Ferranti Thistle player Hugh Cowan. He was twice vice-chairman of Meadowbank Thistle, first under John Blacklaw and later Bill Hunter. Cowan took over from Bill Mill as the club's representative on the East of Scotland Football Association, a position he holds to this day – now representing Livingston FC. He still watches the club's games.

John Blacklaw, the RAF squadron leader, former Ferranti executive and first chairman of Meadowbank Thistle, later became honorary president of Livingston and remained so until he died aged 90 in March 2002.

Yet anther figure of the old days is Robin Melrose who signed for Ferranti Thistle in 1963, having previously played at Dunfermline and also down at Southend United in England. Melrose later became founder member of Meadowbank and is still a Livingston shareholder.

A person whose role in helping turn Meadowbank into Livingston cannot be overlooked is Bill Hunter. Though he attracted controversy and criticism, it was Hunter's vision of a new start for the club that set it off on the road to the success of today. The businessman's connections with the club stretched back to the early 1980s when he sponsored some home games, and continued even after his sold his controlling interest in Livingston in 1998.

There are others still working at Livingston who also have links with the Ferranti and Meadowbank eras. The club secretary Jim Renton was previously a senior referee and was in charge of a number of crucial Meadowbank games over the years; including the match against Brechin City in which they clinched promotion for the first time in 1983. Later, after retiring as a match official, he wrote to a number of football clubs offering his services and Meadowbank took him on. He has been with Thistle and now Livingston for the past decade.

One person at Almondvale, the club's head of security Alistair Hood, saw Ferranti Thistle from the other side. The former senior police officer and ex-head of security at Rangers played for police sides against Ferranti Thistle on many occasions in the 1960s. As a result he knows men such as John Bain well.

Another recruit to Livingston in 1998, former Hearts star John Robertson, also had strong connections with Meadowbank. 'Robbo', who was player/coach then coach, and who is now manager of Caley Thistle, had been a ball boy at Thistle's first ever senior game back in 1974, and his older brother Chris had played for the club in the mid-1980s.

Jim Leishman, the manager, general manager and chief executive of the club over eight and a half years, straddled two different eras in its history. 'Leish' was its last manager as Meadowbank Thistle's and its first as Livingston. He of course has now returned to Dunfermline.

These, then, are some of the people who have provided a connection between the old and new at Livingston; who have maintained its proud links with the past.

There are others now whose job it is to take Livingston into the future. Until recently one of the key people involved in this was of course Dominic Keane, club chairman and the man who – with Willie Haughey – had the vision to see Livingston's potential and rescue it from near-bankruptcy in 1998.

After the main part of this book was written Dominic sadly had to step down as the club went into administration – but his vital role in rejuvenating the club cannot be overlooked or overstated. Another of the men who helped in the resurgence of the club was John McGuinness, Livingston FC vice-chairman, who has become a fan as well as a shrewd and trusted benefactor of the club.

Livingston has also been happy to bring in new blood, people who have helped to take the club to a higher level. These include Charles Burnett who joined as commercial manager Livingston in 1998 after a long spell in a similar role at Hearts. Burnett quickly saw the need to bind the club into the community, with the fans, and also the benefit of tapping into the high-tech industries that have sprung up in the area. His work has helped to ensure that the club has been as successful off the field as it has been on it.

Two more important figures in the present day club are goalkeeping coach Roy Baines and fitness coach George McNeil. Baines played in goal until he was 37, representing Hibernian, Morton, Celtic and St Johnstone. In his time he has coached Scotland 'keepers Rab Douglas and Neil Armstrong. McNeil is not just a fitness fanatic but was a world-class sprinter in his day. Appointed by Jim Leishman, he had been the fitness coach with Hearts when Alex McDonald and Sandy Jardine were in charge. Both Baines and McNeil feel at home in what they see as the 'family atmosphere' of the club.

Indeed, the modern Livingston club is as keen as it was in the days of Ferranti and Meadowbank to maintain a family image. A literal example of this is the Wilson family Bobby, Lorraine, Craig, and Gordon. Bobby is in charge of mascots and ballboys, Lorraine works in the club's office, Craig was once a ball boy, and Gordon is 'Roary', the little lion mascot.

Another example is the Sinclair family; husband Willie is the 'Livi Lion', while his wife Elaine ran the café with their daughter Amy and son Billy, and also helps with the laundry and cleaning. Then there are Kay and Carol Robertson and their daughter Keira. Kay is the club's fans liaison officer and along with Keira is herself one of the keenest of Livingston supporters. Meanwhile Carl, known as Boab, is a serviceman who served in the Gulf, a keen fan and is the club's trumpeter.

Despite its unusual past, the knowledge and passion of Livingston fans compares well with any club in Scotland. Local assistant librarian Jackie Stark, a keen follower of the club with husband Derek, is to be seen at all games, home and away.

Another committed fan is Lorraine Kelly, who has watched the club since Meadowbank days when she was a girl of just thirteen. The affection in which is held was demonstrated after Lorraine suffered the misfortune of being knocked down coming home from a match; well-wishers at her hospital bedside included not just fellow fans but players too. Another stalwart is Davie Lyall who helped drive the coaches when supporters made their long trek to Liechtenstein and Austria for the UEFA Cup games. One of the oldest fans meanwhile is Angus Paton, who while being in his early 80's still makes it to most home matches and some away games too. He is one of the old Meadowbank fans who accept that if Thistle had not changed, they may well have perished.

So despite all the current hardships that Livingston and Scottish football in general face, can the fans of this great club continue to look forward to the future with confidence?

It is true that already in its short history the club has experienced many of the peaks and the troughs that football has to offer. The 2003/4 season alone shows that; the ecstasy of beating Hibs 2-0 to win the CIS Insurance Cup countered by the misery of going into administration.

But look at what progress the club has made. During its time in West Lothian the club has risen to the Premier Division, played European football and established a healthy fan base. Along the way, the club has forgotten neither its roots nor its traditions; and nor will it while there are still men who remember the glory days of the public parks. The Thistle may have changed into a Lion, but the old memories still linger. Fortunate is the club that can look back and look forward with equal pleasure.

This club will survive!